Praise for Lynette Allen

'I always know when I meet someone who is on a mission, destined to do something special. It doesn't happen often but it's exciting when it does. Lynette blew my socks off. I have had the pleasure of working with her a number of times since. Her stature as a leading coach and author working with women grows daily. One of the few coaches I would use myself and happily refer clients to.'

Nic Rixon, founding partner, Shirlaws UK (www.shirlaws.biz) and author of *Design Your Life*

'I'm using *Behind with the Laundry and Living off Chocolate* like a "magic" tool book and literally just pick a chapter once a day to focus and remind me to stay awake and aware. It feels so practical and real.'

Suzy Greaves, life coach and author of *Making the Big Leap* (www.thebig-leap.com)

'I feel *so* much better and more positive about everything, and now that I am focusing my attention … I feel much clearer and much better able to focus on what's important. Thank you so much for your help. You really have been more inspirational than you know!'

Patti Good, journey therapist (www.pattigood.com)

'I feel like I'm letting me be me for the first time in my life and it feels amazing. I am really looking forward to using the motivation technique you suggested, as every time I see the picture in my head, it just fills me up with tears of pride! You have the gift of giving me the tools to make the future bright and happy. I feel relief. Thanks again.'

Kerry McIntosh, managing director, Meeters (www.meeters.co.uk)

'I wanted to say thank you officially for your help. You really have been great and a fund of good advice. I am making a resolution to be more organised and write things down, decide on priorities, review progress etc. I think you have a real talent for your job.'

Mary Walsh, freelance writer

Behind with the Mortgage and Living off Plastic

*Charge up your life,
not your credit card*

Lynette Allen

First published by

Crown House Publishing Ltd
Crown Buildings, Bancyfelin, Carmarthen, Wales, SA33 5ND, UK
www.crownhouse.co.uk

and

Crown House Publishing LLC
4 Berkeley Street, 1st Floor, Norwalk, CT 06850, USA
www.CHPUS.com

British Library Cataloguing-in-Publication Data
A catalogue entry for this book is available from the British Library.

10 Digit ISBN 1904424953
13 Digit ISBN 978-190442495-6

LCCN 2005925550

Printed and bound in the UK by
Cromwell Press, Trowbridge, Wiltshire

For James, The Wonderful Man

The Wonderful Man was strong,
The Wonderful Man was handsome,
The Wonderful Man took you in his arms and made you
feel exactly the way you always wanted to feel.
That is why they called him the Wonderful Man.

From 'The Interesting Thoughts of Edward Monkton' – with sincere thanks

www.edwardmonkton.com

Acknowledgements

My thanks for helping me turn this book from a mere idea over a latte and a muffin in a London Waterstone's Coffee Shop to fully fledged follow-on from *Behind with the Laundry and Living off Chocolate* go to my publisher Caroline Lenton. Her unfailing enthusiasm and trust in my ability inspire me more than she knows.

Special thanks to Fiona Spencer Thomas, my agent and editor, who once again has skilfully helped to keep me focused, making sure that you, the reader, don't have too much waffle to trowel through before you get to the good bits. Thank you, Fiona.

The talented Tom Fitton, as always, pulled out all the stops to design and organise everything for the very glamorous front cover. Unfortunately, at his suggestion, I had the demanding and gruelling job of trying on endless designer dresses at After Dark on the Finchley Road in London (www.eveningwear.me.uk). As you can imagine, it was a tough day, made all the easier, though, by Douglas Griver and his staff, who were marvellously patient with us. We finally chose the most fun dress I've ever worn, from Catwalk Collection. I then had to endure a brilliantly relaxed and fun photoshoot with two other talents, photographer James (www.jamesandjames.net) and makeup artist Paola Recabarren (www.missbingmake up.co.uk) who both made me look flippin' good, even if I do say so myself!

My thanks also go to my extraordinary clients for not only letting me in on their lives and dreams but also for letting me publish their stories. Special thanks to Suzy Greaves, for her kindness and massive generosity. Thank you to the wonderfully energetic and inspirational Nic Rixon, for letting me use one of his most powerful techniques (if you want to know what it is, you'll have to read the book!). Heartfelt thanks to a very special coach and friend, Gabrielle Blackman-Shepphard, for her wonderful insights into the mind of the opposite sex. What a guiding star you are!

Thanks also to my ever-supportive parents, John and Jan, my brother Craig for his witty one-liners (some of which I've stolen!), plus my sister-in-law Tracey and fab friend Lesley for their very generous help. Also, thanks to Denise and Roy Chambers, plus every one of my friends for instilling so much confidence in me. Lastly, thank you to my wonderful husband, the very gorgeous Nick, for putting up with me and for coming up with snappy lines such as 'Your fifties are your twenties with style' and letting me pass them off as my own!

Contents

Introduction

A girl's best friend? Shopping! Did you think it was diamonds? Well, apparently not! More than ever these days when the going gets tough, the tough go shopping. This book isn't about the billions of pounds worth of debt we're supposed to have on plastic – and you won't find anything on the whys and wherefores of the latest ISAs or interest rates. This is about the fundamental stuff that makes us girls go shopping when in crisis (it's amazing how good a Prada handbag can make you feel in the middle of the worst day ever!). Ever wondered if you'd spend as much if everything in your life were rosy? Well the truth is you probably wouldn't. This book isn't just papering-over-the-cracks stuff: it's about getting to the nitty-gritty of our imagined inadequacies, the lack of that certain sparkle that makes us want to add more and more material value to boost our egos, improve our self-confidence and prove our worth, competence, independence and overall success to the whole world and its mother. Maybe diamonds *are* a girl's best friend after all – but only if we've bought them ourselves for ourselves, just because we can!

You don't need to be in debt to get the most from this book. Even the savers among us girls sometimes feel as if life isn't running quite as smoothly or as perfectly as we'd like. If that sounds like you, you won't be able to put this book down. This is pure 'must-have handbag chic' that you'll use time and time again as a crucial aid to getting through impossibly difficult days when nothing else seems to help. You'll get tips on everything from complaining in shops and dealing with depression to revving up your sex life by understanding what language your man really speaks. It's brimming with straight talking, from the heart, practical steps that'll turn you effortlessly from 'crumpled, stressed-out heap on the floor' to 'sassy, elegant woman in high heels and red lipstick who thrives on running the world single-handedly'.

If you're a woman and you're reading this in the bookshop, then you're probably wondering where on earth you'd even fit in the time or enthusiasm to absorb its secrets. Maybe you're wondering whether you'll really find the answers you're so desperately searching for, the answers that every woman dreams she'll just stumble across one day, making everything from housework to cellulite perfect overnight. Maybe you're a man and are wondering whether to buy this for your wife, girlfriend or partner. Mmm, tricky situation, that one. Will you get the

'So you think I can't cope?' look, the 'What's wrong with spending money on myself occasionally?' look? Or will you get the 'This is fantastic, you're so sensitive and I want babies with you' approach! (Sorry, chaps, can't help you there – only one way to find that out!)

If you've already bought this book, however, then I wouldn't be at all surprised if you're squeezing in a few pages before bed until you can't keep your mascara-stained eyes open any longer. Perhaps you're on the train to work, ready to face yet another full-on, anxiety-ridden, twelve-hour day before crawling home exhausted, tired, tearful and asking questions such as, 'Is this all there is?', 'How come life got this tough?' and 'Where did I put my credit card?'

If any of the above is you and you're a woman who works, hosts, looks after, clears up, cleans up, arranges and prepares – just so tomorrow will actually happen – this book is exactly right for you and will help you take the first steps to dragging your soul up from the bottom of your high heels and letting it shine with vitality and energy for everyone to see. These short (yes, I did say short) chapters contain little pieces of information, strategies and tips that all aim to give you the renewed energy you're searching for, the self-confidence you crave and the ability to take on whatever is thrown at you during the day with a newfound sense of calm and control. Sound good? Then this book, I'm sure you'll agree, is what every woman deserves.

The thing is, we women are always searching for perfection. It seems to be our lifelong ambition to do everything really, really well for pretty much all of the time. Perfect mother, perfect partner, perfect employee, perfect daughter – there's all that pressure of being torn between work and home, baking cakes for the children's fête versus scoring points with our boss by staying another hour when everyone else has given up and gone home long ago. Do you take time off when your child is ill? Not a chance! You hurry into work as normal while secretly phoning your babysitter every half-hour, hoping your boss doesn't notice you crouched under your desk as you whisper 'The Calpol's in the second cupboard on the left.' When you're ill, do you give in, turn off the phone and go back to bed, hiding under the duvet with Belgian truffles, menthol tissues and endless cups of tea? Hell, no! You're on that train, looking as stylish as is humanly possible, wearing inch-thick makeup to hide the bags and sucking enough Strepsils to down a herd of charging wildebeest!

There's no doubt life can be very tough and this book aims to be all you ever wanted it to be. *Behind with the Mortgage and Living off Plastic* covers a whole host of scenarios and issues that every woman encounters during the course of her day and it gives you a strategy to deal with every single one. The theory is that, if you get everything in your life running smoothly, you'll be so deeply calm and collected that the desperate need to grab your purse and run screaming down the high street like a woman possessed will become a thing of the past, leaving you more in control of your emotional and financial life than ever before.

You can either read this book cover to cover or dip in and out at whichever chapter seems most appropriate to you at the time. If you're really clever, you'll use that female intuition of yours by closing your eyes, holding the book in your hands, thinking of the issue (or stress!) of the moment, and then opening the book at whatever page feels right. Don't peek, though, and don't try too hard. Just trust that the answers to your prayers will lie wherever you opened the book, and you will be amazed.

All these strategies are already tried and tested by my clients, who have kindly agreed to share their inspirational stories with you. They are normal, everyday women, some with careers, some with families. Some are high flyers, some just want to work to pay the bills. But what I've realised through my work as a professional coach is that it doesn't matter what we do, who we are or who we're perceived to be. The very fact that we're women makes us strong, capable and competent individuals. It's just that sometimes we get so caught up in everyday struggles that we fail to see what wonderful, amazing, talented and beautiful creatures we really are. This book, ladies, is your reminder. Enjoy!

Shopaholics R Us!

Need to get your finances in order? Need to get your spending habits under control? Start today, it's time to be upfront and honest.

When I saw Natalia she was desperately worried about her financial situation. The basic problem was that her earnings didn't cover her expenses and each month she was sinking deeper into debt. She had two credit cards that were nearly full and she was able to pay off only the bare minimum. Every time Natalia felt down about her financial situation, she went shopping to make herself feel better and the emotional 'high' of buying new boots or adding to her CD collection was enough to make her temporarily forget her ever-growing credit card bills. The problem was that the glorious, euphoric shopping moment never lasted long and, by the time the credit card bill dropped through the door again, her self-esteem and confidence plummeted even further.

At that very first meeting with Natalia, I asked her to bring her credit card and bank statements, so we could work out exactly where her wages were going each month.

She knew she had various standing orders going out of her bank account each month but didn't know how *much* they were for, *when* they went out or *what* they were for. Natalia had no idea where she was spending her money, and so the first thing she decided to do was to look at the reality of her situation. She started noting down every time she spent something. Although a portion went on food and petrol, she'd been spending extra money on clothes, CDs, books, meals out with friends, cinema tickets and extravagant presents for friends and family, none of which she could afford. Natalia hadn't realised the extent of her spending until she was forced to look at it on paper.

Natalia had enough CDs and books to open her own shop and many of her clothes hadn't even had the labels removed. She admitted to being addicted to the bargain rail. She just could not walk past a so-called bargain or a two-for-one offer without snapping something up, despite the fact that she didn't need the items. This wasn't just a financial situation, but an emotional one too and if Natalia was to get a grip on her spending, it wasn't just the pennies she had to account for: it was the *underlying reasons* for her overspending that had to be addressed.

On the emotional front, armed with a trusty credit card, Natalia thought anything was possible. She felt powerful and in control of her life, but that was a million miles away from how she told me she felt without her credit card in her back pocket. Without the spending power, Natalia didn't feel successful and she felt less confident about her standing in the world. She said she even walked differently and slouched without its reassuring presence. During that session she realised how strongly she linked money to success, and she realised that, without money, she felt a failure.

The truth was that Natalia had a string of successes behind her: she'd done well at school, despite having had much of her latter years disrupted by ill health; she'd learned to speak several languages for her work; and her colleagues looked up to her and were always asking for her help and advice. Natalia was in fact a strong-minded, capable and intelligent woman who had succeeded where many wouldn't. Until then, she hadn't realised the link that she'd subconsciously made between success and money. She attached a huge emotional value to her credit card and agreed to explore ways of finding other, more positive things to boost her feelings of self-worth.

On a practical level, I asked her what went through her mind when there was no one to police her, when she was standing at the till with her bargains draped over her arm. She said she was usually feeling quite smug about her finds and she'd be busy counting up the money she was saving herself. In the long run though, you save yourself money on sale items *only* if you were going to buy them anyway. Natalia's trick, to avoid the reality of her spending, was to busy her mind while she queued, in order to stop herself from feeling guilty about spending. I asked her if she would have bought those items for the full price and she said, 'Probably not!'

So that was the key to the solution. I asked Natalia to ask herself, when she was next queuing to pay for an armful of 'bargains', 'Would I pay full price for these?'. She agreed to ask herself that question and also agreed to put them back on the rail and walk out of the shop if her answer was 'no'. Remember, a bargain is a bargain *only if you would pay full price for it or planned to buy it anyway.*

Next, we made a list of everything that went out of her bank account each month. She chose to cancel the things that she didn't need or wasn't using. Then we worked out a budget for her to live on that was within her means. That meant writing down everything she needed during the month – petrol to get to work, food, money for bills, rent, insurances and so on. Anything left over would be put into a separate account that would go towards paying off her credit card bills.

The next thing Natalia did was to cut up one of her credit cards. She decided that, as an emergency backup only, she'd keep just one of the cards and agreed to take it out of her purse and put it in a sealed envelope marked with red pen EMERGENCY ONLY.

From now on, she would pay for everything using cash and tell herself that, when her monthly wage was gone, there was no more.

Natalia's plan worked and she got a firm grip on her spending habits. If you're slipping further into debt, follow this three-step plan to making yourself financially secure again.

1. Ask yourself what spending gives you. Is it fun? Is it an energy lift? Is it a social occasion with your best friend? Does it boost your ego? Does it stop you from worrying about other things that are missing in your life? Work out what shopping gives you and write down your answers below.

_____

_____

_____

_____

_____

Next, list here at least five other things that would give you the same feeling. If you're imaginative, there will be numerous other activities that could give you the same 'high' as shopping but without the worry of the monthly bill.

_____

_____

_____

_____

_____

2. Be honest with yourself, admit your financial situation and plan to change it. Have a system for the bills, put them in the same place in the house and remember to check them often so you don't forget to pay them. Save up for quarterly bills by putting a regular small amount

away in a separate account each month. That way, there shouldn't be too many shocks when they arrive. If you're self-employed, keep outgoings, loans and standing orders as low as possible, so you don't need to worry in the quiet months. A great tip is to put by a small amount in your current account as a buffer, just in case a standing order or direct debit goes up before you have adjusted your figures. Become a credit card expert. Ask someone to explain the interest rates to you properly, in plain English, and, if you just can't bring yourself to cut them up, then follow Natalia's lead and seal them in an envelope marked EMERGENCY ONLY. It may just be the deterrent you need next time you've had a bad day and feel a Moschino moment coming on!

3. Don't depress yourself by trailing around the shops looking at things you can't afford. Avoid the sales and decide to do something else more profitable with your time. Flicking through the catalogues that litter your lounge won't help, either: make the decision to close your accounts and throw them away. Lastly, if it's the shopping channel that gets you every time, be brave and organise for it to be disconnected. Paint your toenails red instead; invite a friend over for a face pack/DVD evening; choose to occupy your time differently. You won't even miss it.

Make the decision today to throw away those anxieties about not being good enough or not being able to afford material belongings. Add value to yourself as a person and concentrate your energy on feeling good enough just as you are.

Sexual chemistry

Has your sex life passed its sell-by date? Will you do anything to avoid intimacy? Would you rather dunk a digestive than dip into the Kama Sutra? Ladies, this could help!

It's no secret that men think about sex roughly every thirty seconds. It doesn't seem to matter what they're doing throughout the day, they have sex on their minds for the majority of it. Sex or footie – isn't that what most men are meant to dwell on for 90 per cent of the time? It's also no secret that some women would just rather cuddle up with a good book and a cup of tea than get jiggy with it under the duvet!

Men and women generally want sex for different reasons and it's important to know those reasons. A woman, for instance, generally feels sexy around the time she ovulates – it's a nature thing, it's our way of keeping the population going. It's not that we don't like sex, though: most women adore the intimacy of making love and the sharing and deep connection it gives us, and that bit isn't hugely different from what men want. Yes, they're basically up for it most of the time – but, then, they have to be because we're so unpredictable. Let's face it, we never really know when we're going to feel like it: it could be days, hours or even weeks. A man, therefore, is equipped never to miss his chance. Like buses, we'll either all come at once (excuse the pun!) or he could have to wait around for days. Men use sex to show us how much they love us. It's their way of demonstrating how they feel physically. Now this is the bit where confusion can run wild, communication can stop and couples can start to feel a million miles apart from each other. This is the danger zone – but there is a strategy to help.

Men want us to know they care and they demonstrate that by getting sexy. Women, on the other hand, show their affection by talking, cuddling or kissing. It's just not as important for us to get to the fumbly bit! We class the talking, cuddling and kissing bit as making love, too. We love the intellectual stimulation as well as the physical, and, if we feel that's lacking, there'll be no way our men are going to get to second base! There are tips here for the boys as well as the girls, so, if your man's idea of foreplay is turning off the light, then get him to have a read too.

For the boys

Humour us! Yes, of *course* we want multiple orgasms; yes, of *course* we want to feel the earth move; and yes, we'll make you feel like king of the jungle. But we need something first, and it's not a quick faff around under the sheets, boys! Listen up, because this is the important bit: we need to feel loved, appreciated and cared for, and we know that you really do love us, care for us and appreciate us when you say it and demonstrate it in every way other than sex! Sorry, boys, words as well as actions really do count for a lot, but you'll have to mean it and you'll have to take your time. This is a process that cannot be rushed.

A friend of mine, Gabrielle, once said that looking after a woman is like looking after a plant. You have to give the plant a little bit of water every day. That way the water is absorbed, the plant grows nicely, looks lovely and green and thrives happily in the sun. If, on the other hand, you forget to water the plant for two weeks and then pour half a pint in to make up for it, the water will simply drain straight through the soil, the plant won't be able to take any of it in, will wilt, look very sad and stop growing.

So, if you pride yourself as a bit of a green-fingered god, think about your other half as a plant that needs nurturing with love. Tell her every day that you love her; notice whether she's looking tired and do something to relax her (a decent foot massage goes way further than you think); treat her occasionally and compliment her a lot. And I can guarantee that all will be as you would wish in the bedroom!

For the girls

Remember that sex isn't just sex for men. Sex is their way of showing you they love you and it's important to let them show it. Now, obviously, I'm not talking about giving them their wicked way whenever they demand it. After all, this is the twenty-first century, not the eighteenth. But, if you say no all the time, they'll feel rejected, hurt and alone. If you really aren't up for a night of passion, if you've spent the day struggling round the shops, arguing the toss with the children, have had pressure and targets thrown at you all day at work and have period pains to top it off, then tonight probably isn't the night that's going to rock your world or his.

However, do not – I repeat: *do not* – try to ignore his advances. It's imperative that you don't pretend to be asleep, that you don't turn over and push him away or that you don't start an argument with 'Is that all you ever want?'

There are ways of telling your man he won't be winning any athletic contests that night, and here is the perfect way to do it without hurting his feelings and making him feel unloved and rejected.

When he makes an unwanted advance, tell him you know you haven't had sex for ages, that you still fancy him and adore him and that you will have sex again one day, but that today has been really tough and you just need a cuddle. Turn the bedside lamp on, talk to him, look him in the eyes and be warm and loving. Most men aren't out for what they can get and telling them that they are can make them feel awful. Avoiding the subject altogether is as bad and leaves the floodgates wide open to all kinds of misinterpretation. If you don't explain, he'll be thinking all kinds of things, from the idea that you must be having an affair to the idea that you obviously no longer fancy him. This is about communication, it's about being honest, it's about telling him how much you love him, that there's still no one else for you and that you will feel very sexy again one day soon.

Take the pressure off, be light-hearted about your lack of sex drive when all you can think about are the packed lunches for tomorrow and whether the chicken will defrost in time for dinner. No matter what your ages, a little humour, honesty and communication will give you both back your va-va-voom!

Now this is all assuming that your man can't wait to pounce on you and is constantly trying to laugh you into bed, but what happens if it's your man who's lost his sex drive and it's you who is desperate for some action between the sheets? This is quite serious and more common than you might think. For men to feel sexy, they too need to feel loved, but, above all, they need to feel worthy. Gabrielle Blackman-Sheppard, an executive coach, is passionate about coaching men and says:

> A man needs to feel worthy to initiate sex. In order to feel worthy, he needs to feel he has achieved something important and gained respect. He needs to feel as if he has striven hard for something, been a good father or solved a difficult problem.

These are very 'male' things and, as women, we're very good at underestimating how important these achievements are to men. It's vital for us to be aware that they're of paramount importance if your man is to feel worthy of you and worthy enough to initiate sex.

So how can we help? It's important for us to let him know that he is worthy because of 'who he is' and not because of 'what he does'. It will help if we let him know that the pressure of performing (not just in the sexual sense) can be lifted, that it is his presence that we appreciate and love and not what he can do for us. Gabrielle continues:

> Our man's presence – by which I mean his full presence (gut, heart and soul), not his physical presence while he is watching sport on TV – is so beautiful to us that it has the power to heal our heart. It is such a shame that we don't know how to communicate this to the man we love. He doesn't have to do anything – he just has to be there with us. When a man gets a sense of that, he becomes powerful in a way he never knew possible. That's the miracle of what we can do for him.

If bedroom activities in your house have come to a standstill and your man isn't making any moves, there could be all kinds of reasons. Make sure that when you talk to him you make it clear that you love him and appreciate his presence in your life. This isn't about pandering to 'men's needs'. Women are capable of making men's needs something to laugh at, and jokes about treating them as children are all too common. There is a fine line to be had here and maybe, every so often, we girls could do with taking a look at our behaviour too. We need to respect their feelings just as we demand that they respect ours. All is not lost – try it and see the difference it can make.

A woman's work is never done – or is it?

Do you get lumbered with all the chores in the house? Do you find yourself moaning that you may as well do it because nobody else will? Well take a look at this ...

We've all heard (and maybe even used) the saying 'a woman's work is never done', but this tip may make you think a bit differently. I know I go on about this but I genuinely think women do draw the short straw sometimes. Women get childbirth; men get shaving! Women get careers, housework and bringing up families; men just get careers. Now I am aware that this is a *huge* generalisation, since there are many men in this world who are single parents, bringing up capable and fantastic children, cooking and cleaning as well as supporting their families and doing it brilliantly. In fact, if you're feeling kind of smug right now, it probably means that your partner isn't bad with a feather duster, either. However, in many households, it is still predominately the case that the woman is responsible for the house, the children, the pets, the homework and the dinner, as well as her own career and self-development.

Recently, Kelly told me that her eighteen-month-old son had left a trail of destruction behind him everywhere he went and just how grizzly and unpleasant he had been all day. She also had the builders in, the house was a bomb-site and she had only one room downstairs in which to cook and entertain her little boy – and it wasn't the kitchen. It was clearly going to be one of 'those' days and, with one thing and another, she hadn't managed to get dressed, let alone organise any dinner. She explained how, under-standably, she nearly lost the plot when, upon arriving home from the office, her husband said with genuine surprise at the state of the place, 'What have you been doing all day?' Familiar? I thought so! Well a client of mine, Joanne, has got this totally sussed.

Joanne has a rota system for her children. She has three, two of whom are still living at home. Each day they have mandatory chores to do that they tick off on a board in the kitchen. These include cleaning their rooms, making breakfast in the morning, organising packed lunches for everyone and arranging Mum's first cup of tea (oh, bliss!). As well as those tasks, each child has other jobs to do at some point in the day. Those jobs take into account each child's personality. For instance, one of her children has a great sense of humour and her job is to make Mum laugh at least once during the day. Another child has to phone Grandma for a chat. These jobs are completely inspirational and create a fun household to live in. Because of her system, it also means that, when Mum, who works full-time in a school, gets home, the house is fairly well organised. At the end of the day, when each child has ticked off their daily chores, they get pocket money. Simple.

What Joanne has done brilliantly, is make sure that everyone has a job for which they are responsible. She has handed out the daily tasks that so many mothers find themselves coping with alone and has made sure that she isn't left doing everything. Handing out the boring jobs, such as emptying the dishwasher, reading for ten minutes every evening and feeding the guinea pig, isn't just helping Mum: it also doubles up as a creative way to teach children responsibility and accountability for their actions.

If you're getting lumbered with the responsibility for everything and find yourself taking your plastic friend for a walk as a pick-me-up, put this tip into action today. Which chores could your family start taking responsibility for? What are you prepared to let go and give to someone else?

Designate jobs to other members of your household and take the pressure off yourself.

Now, listen carefully, because delegating chores isn't always simple. If you're the type of person who thinks no one can do a job as well as you, think again. When your children take tasks off your hands, they may miss bits, husbands may not think of hoovering the edges as well as the main walkways, the dusting may not be up for any awards, but they're trying – so praise them and then shut up. No 'buts', no 'next time …' If you're asking your children to help or your husband to pull his weight more, never complain about the standard of their work. If you do, they can't be blamed for shoving the duster in your direction and storming off. Don't be a martyr. Be kind, be patient, let them learn, smile and appreciate.

Apologise first

Do you find it easy to get into arguments? Do you find yourself snapping at the wrong person just because they happen to be there? Use this tip to create a bit of harmony.

Most of us, however well we think we control our stress levels, end up biting someone's head off when the pressure peaks, usually for no good reason. We all have worries, some bigger than others, some more stressful than others. But, if you're being accused of being grumpy, picking pointless arguments and generally blowing your top unnecessarily, then here's what to do.

First of all, take yourself off somewhere and identify the real reason why you're stressed. Make sure you're in a safe and relaxed place and work out what exactly is worrying you most. If you can't put your finger on it straightaway, ask yourself how long you've been feeling stressed and then try to remember what was happening around the time it started. Write down everything that you come up with. Drawing up a definitive list of exactly what pressure you're feeling is helpful for lots of reasons: sometimes things don't seem so scary after all when you see them on paper, sometimes it just helps finally to identify why you're crying all the time.

Next, choose to talk to someone you trust about what's going on in your life. Don't keep things secret – tell someone how worried you are and don't try to cope with everything on your own. There are generally very few people we can call close friends – I mean the kinds of friends you could call at three o'clock in the morning in an emergency. Work out which one of your friends would be best for you to talk to and then ask them if you can have a chat. Tell them you're not turning to them for the answers, just the space to tell someone how you're feeling.

The next part of this tip concerns identifying who you've been taking out your stress on. Has one person borne the brunt of all your angst, or have you been generally miserable with everyone? Write down a list of people you may need to apologise to. Now, before you go turning over the pages very fast because I've mentioned the word 'apologise', this isn't as daunting as you might think. I'm not asking you to pour your heart out to people you work with or those who really wouldn't understand or care: what I'm asking you to do here is apologise first for any future tantrums you may have. You don't have to reason why: you just have to make whoever may get the sharp end of your tongue that day know and understand that it's not personal or directed at them.

Think back to a time when someone took your head off with a hurtful remark or a sarcastic comment. Not nice, is it? So, when you next go to work or when you next see a friend you've been especially difficult with, this is your opening line: 'I know I've been really difficult lately. I'm under a bit of pressure at the moment and if I snap I really do apologise. Please don't take it personally – you haven't done anything wrong.'

Imagine that someone said that to you. What a relief it would be to know that you're not the main reason for someone else's bad mood! The first thing we all think when someone is nasty is that we've done something wrong. It's human nature to think that way. Most people immediately put the pressure and responsibility on themselves. Explain that you're going to try not to snap, but, if you do, it's not directed at them personally and they haven't done anything wrong.

This tip worked very well for Annie. Annie was having a really horrible time at work. She was aware that everyone around her was acting differently. People weren't quite so relaxed with her, members of staff were making mistakes, some of which had meant that Annie had had some serious explaining to do to her bosses. Things at work just didn't feel right and she enlisted my help to come in and coach her team to try to bring back the equilibrium.

I went in and spoke to her group, all of whom were lovely, but she was right: the office didn't feel totally relaxed or happy, and there did seem to be a kind of tension in the air. During one of my conversations with Annie she confided that, several months before, at the time when her mother had been diagnosed with cancer, she'd had an argument with her sister. This was clearly and understand-ably the cause of Annie's stress. When I asked what support she was getting and whom she was talking to, she told me that usually it would be her sister, except that her sister had taken the news so badly that she hadn't felt able to cope with their mother's illness. Consequently, they had fallen out and hadn't spoken since.

Annie had always been very close to her sister but, given the fact that they weren't speaking, she had been coping with the strain of everything completely on her own. She felt let down and overwhelmed with the stress of running her mother to hospital, being with her during her treatment and running her office as well. Much as her husband had been brilliantly supportive, she told me she had lost her cool a couple of times at work, and once she admitted that she realised that it may be *her* stress that was rubbing off on her staff and coworkers.

Annie didn't want her family problems to be the subject of office gossip but she did say that she would explain to her staff that she'd been under a lot of pressure and that, if she was short with anyone, it probably wasn't their fault. Any morning when Annie felt particularly upset, she would apologise to people in advance.

I revisited Annie's office a week later and was delighted to see (and feel) a very different atmosphere. Everyone was far more relaxed, mistakes weren't being made and the office was running better than it had done in months. On top of that, Annie had made a date to meet her sister to make things up.

Jo also used this strategy at work. When I met Jo for the first time, she came across as a kind, considerate person who was very easy to talk to. Apparently, this wasn't how she was seen by her colleagues and bosses at work. During one particularly upsetting appraisal, her boss called her 'unapproachable'. Jo never takes her personal life into work but had been going through a really difficult time and knew that she hadn't been easy to work with as a result. We talked through the 'apologise first' strategy, which she enthusiastically put into practice the following week and I received this email from her:

> The best strategy you gave me was to call in my PA when I was having a bad day and tell her that if I was abrupt, to please not take it personally and that I didn't have to explain the problem to her. The result was that she took extra special care of me, brought me tea, took my calls and dealt with any non urgent issues rather than interrupt me. She was so great that amazingly, it turned out to be a good day after all.

What an incredible email to receive first thing on a Monday morning!

Stress and worry – about everything from struggling finances to poor health – are a part of life, and to assume we can eradicate them completely is probably wishful thinking; but it is important not to let them rule your life. Identify what exactly is causing the most stress, talk to someone you trust about how things are affecting you and apologise first to innocent bystanders. Make sure you have the support you need in stressful times and use this tip to control the ripple effect on the rest of your life.

I'm spending because ...

Are you a spender or a saver? How do you react in stressful situations? Do you use shopping to make yourself feel better? Consider the scenarios below and answer as honestly as you can to discover if you're using money as an emotional crutch.

Spending is fab, isn't it? That dizzy buzz we get when we hit the shops with money to burn and a million and one things to buy! There are this season's must-haves, last seasons sales, new lipsticks, foundations, perfumes and eye creams – the list is endless and we want it all. It's an emotional high that every one of us has felt at some point. It's so much fun – and why *shouldn't* we let the moths out of the purse occasionally? After all, life is for living and we can't take it with us, so what's the problem with splashing out sometimes and treating ourselves? Nothing at all. I have no arguments with that whatsoever, just as long as you're not using spending to meet emotional needs that aren't being met any other way! That's the danger.

Every one of us has emotional needs. We all need to feel loved and need our actions to be approved of by our friends and family. We all love to be in control and to feel secure in our relationships. This chapter is about making you aware of those emotional needs. It will help you to decide whether those needs are being met or whether you're desperately trying to nurture them in other, less healthy, ways. Yep, you've got it – by spending!

Unmet emotional needs create huge voids if they're left unresolved, and there are any number of fake ways to feel as if they're getting filled. Working too hard, overeating and overspending are all signs that you're employing alternative, second-rate ways of feeding those emotional needs, and you may not even realise you're doing it.

If, after doing this exercise, you recognise that you're using money as a crutch, then you need to take a closer look at what's lacking in your life that makes you want to seek comfort and stability from possessions.

How you react in stressful or worrying situations gives a lot away about how you meet your emotional needs. Is there always more month at the end of the money? Do you constantly live off your overdraft and find yourself regularly caught out by unexpected bills? If the answer is yes to those questions, it could be that you're using money to satisfy your needs and not facing the reality of your situation. It's crucial to get to the root cause of emotional turmoil before it takes over your life and your bank balance.

I've developed a set of scenarios to help you understand how you react in certain situations. This may give you, in black and white, the proof you need that you'd rather throw money at an event or situation than take the time to deal with it head on. If you've answered this quiz honestly, you'll be giving yourself the chance to see reality at its starkest. It's entirely possible to see what we *should* do in certain scenarios, but I want you to consider what you really *would* do, which is sometimes totally different.

Don't forget that these answers are your own. They're not for other people's eyes. You don't have to tell anyone what you put down. But you *do* have to promise to be *honest with yourself* and have the guts to front up if you use money to paper over emotional craters. So here goes. Take a deep breath and remember to go for the most honest answer.

1. You've just had the day from hell. You're leaving the office, hungry and cold, when you realise there's no food in the house. You nip into the nearest super-market with the intention of buying dinner but mysteri-

ously find yourself in the clothes section, choosing a new pair of shoes to make yourself feel better – after all, you deserve it!

☐   *Yes, I would do that*

☐   *I have been known to do that occasionally*

☐   *No, I wouldn't do that*

2. You've just had an argument with your best friend and you're to blame. You're really sorry and need to apologise, so you call your favourite florist and get them to send her *the* biggest bouquet of flowers. That way, she'll definitely know how sorry you are.

☐   *Yes, I would do that*

☐   *I have been known to do that occasionally*

☐   *No, I wouldn't do that*

3. Your partner says it's over. You're hurt and angry, so you drag one of your friends to town, buy yourself those boots you've had your eye on and treat your friend to dinner in the most expensive restaurant your joint account will allow. You deserve the compensation!

☐   *Yes, I would do that*

   ☐   *I have been known to do that occasionally*

   ☐   *No, I wouldn't do that*

4. You've worked late every evening for the past week. You've missed the children's sports day and your partner's birthday, but it's OK, because you intend to take them away for the weekend to make up for it.

   ☐   *Yes, I would do that*

   ☐   *I have been known to do that occasionally*

   ☐   *No, I wouldn't do that*

5. You're in the job of your parents' dreams and they constantly tell you how proud they are and brag about your success at every opportunity. The problem is you hate going into work each day but reason that it does give you a car to be proud of and a salary to match, so you decide to stay for now.

   ☐   *Yes, I would do that*

   ☐   *I have been known to do that occasionally*

   ☐   *No, I wouldn't do that*

6. It's Christmas time and you need to buy a present for friends who always show off about money. You're fed up of feeling inferior, so you buy them an extravagant present on the credit card. You don't have the finances to pay for it now but you'll sort it in the New Year – it'll be fine.

   ☐ *Yes, I would do that*

   ☐ *I have been known to do that occasionally*

   ☐ *No, I wouldn't do that*

7. Your children pester you for an expensive game that all their friends have. You want them to fit in, despite your being unable to afford it, so you tell yourself they're young only once and end up finding the money from somewhere. After all, you want to be the best mum in the world!

   ☐ *Yes, I would do that*

   ☐ *I have been known to do that occasionally*

   ☐ *No, I wouldn't do that*

8. You've just had *the* most fantastic news and need to celebrate now, so you take your friends out to dinner and treat them to only the best champagne.

☐   *Yes, I would do that*

☐   *I have been known to do that occasionally*

☐   *No, I wouldn't do that*

9. You're worried about your health. You've not felt right for a while and are worried it could be serious. Fearing the worst, you forget all about it and treat yourself to that expensive dress you've had your eye on.

☐   *Yes, I would do that*

☐   *I have been known to do that occasionally*

☐   *No, I wouldn't do that*

10. If you're totally truthful, you're not 100 per cent happy in your relationship, you have a good standard of living though, and your partner never moans when you buy new things, so you stay.

☐   *Yes, I would do that*

☐   *I have been known to do that occasionally*

☐   *No, I wouldn't do that*

Now add up your answers and see how you handle your emotional needs.

Mostly 'yes'

Are you shocked or did you know that money is one of the most important things in your life? You use money on a regular basis to make things OK. You probably know in your heart of hearts that money doesn't get you every-where, but you're determined to see just how far it *does* get you. If you've answered this honestly and you find yourself in this category, well done! It's as good as standing up and shouting 'My name is ___ and I'm a shopaholic!'

Don't look at this result negatively: it could well turn out to be the most positive thing you've done all year. Work out what's really missing in your life and how you can close the gap without using money. If you think your relationship is the problem, then 'Terms and conditions' might be a helpful chapter to read (see page 81). It will give you a tool to get closer to your partner and may well fill a rela-tionship void. On the other hand, if it's the lack of a relationship that's getting to you then 'The dating game' on page 170 should get you feeling totally confident about strutting your stuff again and finding Mr Right. If your self-confidence is low and clothes are the only thing that you trust to make you feel good, reading about Josie's story in 'Radiating gorgeousness!' (see page 121) couldn't be more uplifting. There are all kinds of things that might make you spend excessively but don't be dragged down each month: be your own success story and decide to get financially fit and emotionally strong.

Mostly 'occasionally'

OK, you have a tendency on occasions to cover up emotional problems with money. Realise what you're doing though and next time you find yourself at the counter with your credit card ask yourself, 'Am I spending because I feel down?'. Answer that question honestly and your conscience will tell you whether you need to back away from the counter, go home, lie down in a dark room and work out what you're lacking instead. You might find that you need a Fairy Godmother, as Kerry did in 'Fairy godmothers really do exist' (see page 75) to give you a quick nudge when your resolve gets weak. Maybe it's Natalia's trick of keeping the credit card under lock and key that'll be your inspiration in 'Shopaholics R Us!' (see page 7). Your willpower is strong and you're generally confident in that big wide world. Just remember to keep it that way.

Mostly 'no'

Good news! You're not using money as your emotional crutch. You'd rather tackle a situation head on than leave it festering and you cannot be bought with expensive gifts. While you love to treat yourself and your family now and again, you have the situation well under control. You probably epitomise the 'Ultra-organised divas' (see page 61) perfectly and I'd imagine that you breeze through life not letting too many things get to you. Well done you!

Reality check

If one thing's gone wrong, is the whole day a write-off? Does every month seem to be a bad one? Well try having a closer look and you might be surprised.

It's really easy when something goes wrong to assume that the *whole day* is going to be bad as a result, that it's an omen of some kind that clouds the rest of the day. I wonder why we never think to ourselves, 'Blimey that was a bad hour – never mind, we're in another hour now!'. It's much easier to remember the awful things that went wrong during the month instead of the things that went brilliantly. Some might say it's even more interesting to sympathise with a friend and say that you've had an awful week – just like them. After all your friend won't want to know about your amazing week if her life is falling apart, will she? Whatever the reason, if you focus on the negative all the time, you'll start to believe it. If you tell everyone life is 'awful' or 'dreadful', it will literally alter your view and judgement of the good things and, before long, 'awful' will be your prime response to 'How's life?', not great if you're trying to live life with enthusiasm and not great if you want to be an interesting and fun person to be around.

During one of our coaching sessions, Gillian realised that, given the choice, she'll always err on the negative rather than the positive. She's becoming much more aware of how and when she uses negative language and she's turning her life around as a result. What she realised during one of our sessions is that, whenever anyone asks her how her week has been or how things are going in general, her standard answer seems to be, 'Awful!'

When we talked about it, she realised that she has a habit of focusing on the few awful days in the month and proceeds to tar the others with the same brush, even though the reality is that there have been some great days sprinkled in there as well. When I asked Gillian how she could stop herself focusing on the negative and evaluate her week differently, she came up with a brilliant idea. She now gives herself a daily reality check. At the end of each day, Gillian writes down one word in her diary to describe how the day has gone and she's finding that the majority of her days actually range within the 'OK/good/great' region. Not a bad place to be. Now, whenever anyone asks how she's doing, she replies, 'Great!'

It's true that some days aren't always brilliant. In fact, we all have days when we probably should have stayed in bed. This tip is not about walking around pronouncing that the world is in perfect harmony. Sometimes it's far from perfect, but it's because of the lows we live through that we get to appreciate the highs. It's important to give yourself a reality check and stop letting a few bad days ruin your perception of your whole month.

Gillian even took this tip a stage further. During a subsequent coaching session, while she had a few 'great' days in her diary that month, most were just 'good' or 'OK'. What Gillian was finding was that sometimes she found it hard to actually evaluate what had been a 'good' day, a 'bad' day or a 'great' day. Her mood changed daily depending on all kinds of things – from what she'd eaten to how tired she was. She was keen to put a structure in place that reminded her exactly what a great day was even when she was exhausted with barely enough energy to think, let alone scrutinise what kind of day it had been. So we put together a chart for her to check through. Now this may sound like a whole lot of work and not very exciting but you should see Gillian's chart on the next page – it's inspired!

In the left-hand column, Gillian listed all the achievements that defined a truly great day. At the end of each

Gillian's chart

Achievement	Monday	Tuesday	Wednesday	Thursday	Friday	Saturday	Sunday
I exercised	✓						
I drank plenty of water	✓						
I had no alcohol	✓						
I didn't buy something I didn't need	✓						
I spent quality time with my husband							
I gave myself a treat	✓						
I did some housework, such as hoovering/ dishwasher/kitchen floor and surfaces							
I laughed at least once!	✓						

Example of a 'good' day

day she would place a tick next to each statement that she felt she'd fulfilled that day. Gillian decided that a 'great' day would have 7 ticks or more, a 'good' day 3–6 ticks and a 'bad' day less than 3 ticks.

As you can see Gillian's ideas for a great day are just that – great! Laughing at least once for instance, having quality time with her husband and allowing herself a treat are all important to her. Gillian now has a chart to measure exactly what a 'great' day looks like. Feeling inspired? What would your great-day chart look like? If you could describe a truly fantastic day, what would have to have happened? Perhaps you would have achieved the top three things on your to do-list, saved up for one year's car tax instead of six months' or did a saintly extra five minutes on the treadmill.

Be realistic and look at the things you do in your everyday life that make you feel exhilarated. Do bear in mind here that the emphasis is very definitely on 'you'. What can 'you' do to make sure it's been a great day. Remember that *you're* in control, so don't make others responsible for your happiness. You can't put items on the list for other people to achieve. This is *your* chart and has to detail *your* actions.

What is it that means you come home bursting with excitement and energy despite having run around like a headless chicken all day? Make up your own chart overleaf and fill in the blanks. Next time you need some evidence that life is pretty good, just have a look at your chart!

Achievement	Monday	Tuesday	Wednesday	Thursday	Friday	Saturday	Sunday

Decisions, decisions ...

Are you fed up with making decisions? Do you worry over 'should be simple' day-to-day choices? Are you constantly asking for everyone else's opinion? Time to trust your own decisions.

When was the last time you had to make a major decision? Do you remember what it was about? Think for a second. How did you finally make that decision? Did you go around asking all your friends and colleagues what they would do? Did you use the classic 'A friend of mine has a dilemma' approach? What conclusion did you come up with and what influence were your friends' and family's opinion on that decision? Did it turn out to be the right or the wrong one? This strategy gives you the opportunity to make dithering a thing of the past. From now on, make decisions faster, with a deeper sense of clarity and be certain that you're making the right choice for you.

When we ask others what they would do in our situation, we're after solutions – hand-made, easy-to-pick-up solutions about how to get ourselves out of uncomfortable situations. Sometimes, it'll be a trivial thing and someone else's input can give you a suggestion you may never have thought of before. Other decisions you're going to have to make though will be much more serious, life-changing or personal to you, and no amount of input from anyone else is going to make it easier to decide.

Some decisions you'll have to make very quickly, and asking lots of people for their take on your situation isn't always the best way of approaching your problem. It may even confuse you more. People have such different beliefs, views and experiences that their lives and the decisions they would make have very little to do with your situation. Even though we may see our friends as being like us, we can never view things in exactly the same way. Don't you remember giving a friend advice and being completely sure that, if only they took your advice, their problem would be solved? Well I'm guessing that they didn't take your advice or, if they did, it wasn't the right choice for them.

What someone else would do in your situation could be very different from what you would do. Here are three steps to help you trust yourself to make the right decision and to be able to stand by that decision with conviction.

1. What do you know?

2. What are your feasible and realistic options?

3. What is your intuition telling you?

1. What do you know?

Ask yourself what you already know about your situation and the decision you need to make. Write down the facts, not imagined consequences or worries about the future, just the actual facts surrounding the situation. If, for instance, your decision was based on your job, your 'what-do-I-know?' list could look like this:

1. I am unhappy in my job.

2. I am a qualified accountant.

3. I know I want more excitement and adventure in my life.

_____

_____

_____

_____

_____

2. What are your feasible and realistic options?

The second thing to do is assess what your realistic options could be and your list could look something like this:

1. I could retrain to do something completely different.

2. I could work out exactly how much money I need per month and may be able to take a pay cut while I retrain.

3. I could decide to use my accountancy skills in a different way.

You needn't have just three options: the example above is just to illustrate the point. List as many options here as you can think of. Write down outlandish ones, daft ideas as well as sensible options. This is your chance to come up with an idea you may not have thought of or taken seriously before, and the option that might work may well be way down on the list, so keep scribbling away.

_____

_____

_____

_____

_____

3. What is your intuition telling you?

The third part is to look at your options and take note of how you feel when you read each one. Do you feel excited? Scared? Nervous? Is there one that your eyes keep going back to, reading over and over again? If there are some definite no-nos on the list, cross them off, take a serious look at each of the remaining options and imagine that you've taken that option already. Envisage yourself six months down the line and ask yourself how life feels. This will give you a good indication of what your intuition is trying to tell you. This is a totally safe environment in which to test out some of your options before you do anything drastic. Listen to your intuition and, even if the option you're leaning towards isn't the sensible one, do some research into it. Take a leap of faith if you feel you should, but listen to what your heart is telling you, trust that you're doing the right thing. The only person who will really understand the right choice is you.

The source of bad decision making comes when we:

- worry too much about the consequences of everything we do;
- forget to listen to our intuition; and
- deny ourselves the proper information and options.

Sadly, we're not blessed with the gift of foresight, so give yourself a break, stop regretting your actions and accept that we can make our decisions only on the information we have to hand right now. We only have the options that we allow ourselves at that moment and we have only that gut instinct, that intuitive feeling to help guide us in the right direction.

Use this three-step plan to make the right decision every time and you need never regret anything ever again.

Self-sabotaging?

Are you a person who naturally thinks negatively? Are you envious of those around you who seem to get everything they want when good stuff never happens to you? Well, you could be a serial self-saboteur. Don't worry – this tip is the cure!

A person who self-sabotages is someone who thinks negatively about themselves, those around them and their situation. They are quite often oblivious of the fact that, by being negative, they're hindering their personal development, happiness and chances of professional success. Some of my clients have quite happily admitted that their glass is always half empty. 'I know it should be half full,' they say, but choosing to turn everything towards the positive is not just a hobby for happy people with no problems. This is serious business and, once you're aware of the implications that your negative outlook has on your life, you'll have the tools to do something about it. You can start today.

We all think negatively sometimes. After all we're only human, but if you're thinking negatively for most of the time, you put yourself in victim mode. Why does it always happen to me? How come I never get anywhere in life? I'm just not a lucky person! These are just some of the things you probably say to yourself often. When people put themselves in victim mode, they fail to take responsibility for the situations they find themselves in – it's always someone else's fault. The point is that most of us have ended up in the job we have, in the relationship we have, in the house we live in and our financial situation because, at some point, whether we realised it or not, we engineered it that way. At some point, we chose those things, and, once people realise that they have the power to make their own choices, they take responsibility for their actions and start to dictate their own future.

When people have choices, they can make decisions – good decisions – concerning both their daily lives and their future. Once they start making decisions for themselves, they are able to justify the outcome and take responsibility for it rather than allowing themselves to be at the mercy of others' decisions.

A client of mine, Julie, came to me because she was in a job with no prospects. Her parents had suggested that she work in an office when she left school and, twenty years later, she was still there in that same office, doing the same job with the same people and feeling completely trapped. During our coaching sessions, Julie began to realise that she had been a self-saboteur. She viewed her situation and her job negatively, and, as a consequence, her confidence suffered. Many years ago she had come to the conclusion that she would never get another job.

She also realised that, even though working in an office had not been her idea, she made the decision to go along with her parents' suggestion all those years ago. Once she realised that, she felt she could choose to make another decision – and she did. Julie decided to leave her job and now works for herself as a virtual personal assistant. She took what she was good at, what she knew, and worked out how she could use her skills to improve her life. She was good at secretarial work but craved a challenge, a different working environment, and decided to work from home. That way she controlled whom she worked for, how many hours a day she worked and how much she charged for her time.

Try this test to find out if you are naturally a positive or negative thinker.

What does this say?

OPPORTUNITYNOWHERE

If you think it says 'opportunity nowhere', you are naturally inclined to be a negative thinker.

If you think it says 'opportunity now here', you are naturally inclined to be a positive thinker.

If you've spent most of your life thinking negatively and believing that you are unable to achieve great things, it's going to take more than a half-hearted five minutes to make an impression on your subconscious mind and change your luck, but don't think it can't be done. It can – and here's how.

The first thing you need to do is learn to take notice of your thoughts. What kind of things do you say to yourself? Are you unkind to yourself when you look in the mirror? Do you tell yourself you're stupid? Make a concerted effort to replace your negative self-talk with positive alternatives. Whether you believe it or not is immaterial. Give yourself a positive alternative over and over again. The more times you see it, think it and say it, the more likely it will be that your subconscious will take notice and you'll be living in a positive way, able to achieve the things you want.

People who don't self-sabotage trust their decisions. They have confidence in their ability to live their dreams and to change their habits for the better. People who achieve do so because they believe they can. It's as simple as that. They have to know where they want to go in the first place and what they actually want to achieve. Then, step by step, they do what it takes to make sure they get there. These steps can involve making practical moves such as phoning people, educating themselves or widening their social circle, but they are also working on their minds at the same time. They are positive people who think themselves worthy of success. They praise themselves for achieving the smaller goals that mean the bigger landmarks are in sight. It's not about showing off or telling all and sundry how great you are: it's about having quiet confidence in yourself, knowing that you're on the right track and that you will get exactly where you want to be.

Make a list below of the five most negative things you say to yourself and then write a positive substitute underneath. As always, remember that this is your chance to be completely honest with your answers, since no one else is going to see them.

1. Negative _____

   Positive _____

2. Negative _____

   Positive _____

3. Negative _____

   Positive _____

4. Negative _____

   Positive _____

5. Negative _____

   Positive _____

Make a promise to turn your life around and start by repeating your positive statements every single day, as many times as you remember.

Ultra-organised divas

Are you spending more time panicking than planning? Do you find it difficult to sit yourself down and take stock of a situation sensibly? You're not alone: there are millions like you. But that's no excuse now you have this strategy.

If you worry because your boss has a tendency to look frustrated and the general vibe around the office is that he or she is likely to explode with rage at any given moment, you'd be forgiven for not being able to think straight with fear, but this strategy could be the one that frees your conscience and calms the climate. The tip is to use this to get more organised, take stock of the situation and get it under control. It is a myth that all women are born with that fantastic 'multitasking gene' and can swing it into action at the push of a button. Just because we're women, it does not necessarily mean that multitasking comes easily and that remembering every small detail is a breeze. It's something that has to be learned and, when you know that, you'll also know that your first lesson in becoming an ultra-organised diva has just begun.

If you're forgetful, disorganised and feel under tremendous pressure to get 'it' right, whatever 'it' is, or you think you were on a coffee break when the multitasking gene was being handed out, this is the strategy for you. Be prepared for a complete life change.

This strategy worked really well on Jenny. Jenny is a wife and working mother of two who was in the middle of heading up a major project at work when we met. Her work project also meant she would have to relocate her whole family to the other side of the country. The decision had been made and the process was just starting when she came to me for coaching. With two major events happening at the same time, one in her work life and one in her personal life, the normally very capable and reasonable Jenny was slowly reaching screaming point as changes loomed ever closer.

She had no concept at all of how this would affect her family and how she was going to cope with being the one in control of both projects. Close to tears for much of the day and yelling at the children for going out in odd socks, Jenny realised she needed to get things in perspective.

This should have been an amazingly exciting time for her and her family. The children were looking forward to having a new house, because she had promised them they could decorate their own bedrooms, and her husband worked from home, which meant that he could live anywhere in the country without disruption. The move itself would also take her nearer to her home town, which she missed dreadfully, so why was this draining so much of her energy and time? 'I'm telling everyone I'm so busy at the moment but in actual fact I'm not: this is just the planning stage, and I can't bring myself to do any planning,' she confessed during her first session. 'Instead, I'm wandering round in a mild panic, worrying about how I'm going to cope with it all!'

Jenny urgently needed some structure and a plan of action, so I asked her to write two lists. The first list would detail everything that would need to be done in order to make her project at work run like clockwork. The second list would detail every single step needed to make sure that her house move went without a hitch. These lists involved writing down who she needed to phone, information she needed to gather, letters that needed to be written and sent and decisions that needed to be made – absolutely everything, right down to the very smallest detail.

This may sound like a mammoth task in itself but, once Jenny had her list of things, far from being overwhelmed, she felt a strange sense of calm wash over her, accompanied by a very broad smile. She knew this was the first step towards making everything fall into place. The next part of the process was to ask Jenny to come up with a deadline for each part of the plan, a date of completion for each item.

We then rearranged both lists into order of priority, after which Jenny got out her diary and chose a convenient day and time in which to schedule each detail. Prioritising meant that Jenny knew exactly what needed to be done and in what order she needed to do the jobs. She also had everything scheduled in her diary, meaning that on each day she had just two or three tasks to complete and she also no longer had to feel guilty about not wrapping up the whole thing by this time next week. Jenny now knew that absolutely everything was going to get done calmly, smoothly and – best of all – on time.

Try this with whatever situation you have to tackle. It doesn't need to be as life-changing as moving house – it could be planning for Christmas or organising your family holiday. Whatever it is, once you have your list of jobs together with their deadlines, cut it up (the most satisfying part) and rearrange it in date order. Go through each item on the list, putting a date in your diary when you intend to do that particular job.

Now the secret trick of this exercise is to avoid over-loading yourself with unrealistic and unachievable lists. The whole point of the exercise is to give yourself just a couple of jobs each day. The unexpected will happen and this plan gives you space to deal with the unforeseen when it arrives. Spread your tasks out evenly and every day will turn into the kind of day that means you go to bed grinning instead of grimacing.

Not only does this organise the most fuddled of brains brilliantly, it makes your workload clearer, more concise and much easier to manage. Instead of thinking you have 10 million things to do by the end of the day, you will have cut your list down into bite-sized, easy-to-swallow chunks. If you know your tendency is to hit the shops as opposed to getting more organised, then hide the plastic and try this strategy. Work through your list and tick things off as you go for that really smug glow!

Decluttering commitments

Are you finding yourself emotionally buried under a heap of commitments? Don't want to come across as 'the woman who can't cope'? Worry no longer – there's no need.

We've all been practising decluttering for years now. It's in every magazine we pick up and on every television makeover show there is. We're constantly told to declutter our environment in order to feel calm and in control of our lives and, it has to be said, I'm decluttering's biggest fan. But when was the last time you decluttered your commitments?

It's incredibly easy to take on more and more, everything from small favours for other people to that ever-growing list of pressures we put on ourselves – just so we can praise ourselves for becoming superwoman overnight. The truth is that, for a start, we can't be superwoman all of the time; and, second, if we pretend to be superwoman all the time, others start to believe in the whole myth and assume that we can handle more and more every day. If you're getting bogged down under the pressure of all the things you've committed yourself to, if you get in the car and can't remember where you're meant to be driving, which child-minder the kids are with today and whether you'll be home in time to put the rubbish out, then take a breather, look closely at what you've committed yourself to and make a huge list.

Now be warned: this list *will* be scary! If you've got to the hysteria stage, it's because the list has got way too much to handle, so breathe in deeply (with or without a glass of wine), take a pen and paper and list everything that you've promised to do for everyone – everything from car sharing to cooking for friends, from standing in for colleagues at meetings to singlehandedly organising the school fête.

Take another deep breath and look at the first item on the list. First, do you really, really want to do it? Second, do you have time, anyway? Be strict and honest with your-self here because putting other people first is how you got here. Don't even think about how you're going to turn that person down at the moment. Just answer the questions 'Do I want to do it?' and 'Do I have the time?' Put a tick for 'Yes, I'll keep it in' and a cross for 'No, it's got to go'. Work on the basis that at least one half of your list must go.

Lisa started one of her coaching sessions in tears as she told me how stressed she felt and how even the slightest problem could turn her whole house into total chaos. By her own admission she was really starting to feel that she was losing her grip on reality. A woman on the edge, she reeled off the huge list of everything she had committed herself to do. It was no wonder she was sinking under the pressure, but she did manage to laugh when she told me she couldn't even go to the loo without rescheduling something.

When life gets this hectic (and we girls seem to be programmed to make it that way) it's time to re-evaluate how you want to live, how your commitments may be affecting your health and your sense of humour, what is really important to keep and what you can let go. This isn't about being selfish: this is about demanding your right to live in a calmer and more 'together' world (and, by the way, know this: the person in charge of this calmer and more 'together' world is you!). This is important stuff. You're important – too important – to be walked over by well-meaning friends who assume that your load isn't as big or important as theirs. I asked Lisa to write down her list of commitments and we talked through each item one by one. She agreed to cancel three of her commitments that day and, following the inevitable discussion about how to let those people down gently, I suggested that it was really important not to make up fake excuses but to be totally truthful with friends and colleagues and let them know that you've taken on more than is humanly possible.

When people see that you're not walking around in superwoman's outfit they'll start to ask before they assume next time, giving you the chance to decline politely. By just lifting those three things off her shoulders, Lisa felt that everything else was more manageable.

What's your commitment list looking like? Don't get lulled into the false belief that you have to carry out *everything* you're committed to. Sometimes it's OK to be honest and say, 'Life's just got too hectic!'

Contingency planning

Worrying about things that haven't happened yet? Maybe you're in a situation that could go two ways and are stressing over the consequences? Take control of any situation by having a secret contingency plan all of your own.

OK, you needn't tell anyone about this contingency plan. It's all yours, your very own peace of mind when everything in your world is not going according to plan.

When we're stuck in the middle of a situation we don't like, we don't always feel in control and, when we feel the control slipping, we're likely to take out our frustrations on that credit card and spend for Britain. We have to face the reality that other people make decisions that affect our lives all the time and sometimes we have little control over their choices. Instead of worrying about what others will decide and what you're going to do if it all goes against you, construct a secret back-up plan to make sure that even if the worst happens, you know you're covered. With a well-thought-through contingency plan you'll have the comfort of knowing that, whatever happens, you're going to be OK. It means that you're far less likely to be taken by surprise, because you'll already be two steps ahead.

Juliette did this when we talked about her relationship with her partner. Just months after giving birth to their beautiful baby daughter, Juliette realised her relationship wasn't as solid as she had hoped it was, and that she and her partner were considering separating. The worry about how she would cope meant that those early months with her baby were filled with unsettled emotions and Juliette wanted to feel calmer to avoid letting her baby sense her fears. If they separated, Juliette was all too aware that she would have to rearrange everything from finances to childcare and she didn't feel able to do it alone. She decided that the only way to control her anxiety was to feel more prepared, so we decided to get her a contingency plan. I asked Juliette a few questions including the following.

- If you were to separate tomorrow, what would need to be done first?

- What would be the worst thing that could happen and how would you handle that?

- What alternative childcare arrangements could you make?

- How much money do you actually need to bring in each month?

- How would you need to rearrange your finances?

- What legal advice would you need?

Once we went through these questions together, Juliette realised that, although it would be far from ideal, if the worst happened, there would be very little to rearrange. She had managed to work and run her own house before and, with a little help from friends and a childminder who had been recommended, she was pretty sure she could be a single parent too. Her mum had brought her up as a single parent and had been a strong and independent lady, so Juliette took strength from that and decided that, if necessary, *she* could do it.

Knowing what she was going to do if her relationship failed meant that the fear had been taken out of the threat and she felt in control again. Since Juliette started to feel back in control, both she and her partner have been working together on rebuilding the trust and strength in their relationship and are now getting married.

Another client who was growing more concerned by the day was Emily. She had a burning ambition to become a vet. In the last year of her A-levels, the stress was starting to show. Being a vet was all that Emily had ever dreamed of and, for her, there was just no other option, it was that or fail. Consequently, the pressure on her to excel was mounting.

The problem was that Emily was working as hard as she could. Not only was she studying, but she ran a vets' society twice a week at school and also did work experience once a week. She would fall asleep reading her books, would study before leaving for school in the morning and was taking no time to relax or spend time with her friends. Her patience was thin and she was tearful, so I asked her to tell me exactly what she would do if she didn't get the results she needed. I asked her to consider if there were other ways of becoming a vet or if she would like to take a year out to assess her situation. This got Emily thinking differently and she looked into other ways of qualifying. In other words, she looked into preparing a contingency plan.

The next time I saw Emily, she glided into my room, smiling from ear to ear. 'I found it!' she laughed. Emily had found a school in Denmark where she could train. She explained that Denmark had a different scoring system from England and she felt confident she could achieve the requirements. Far from being the softer option, it meant that she would have to study for her degree in Danish! This didn't even faze Emily. She was totally excited by the prospect and she found out that the university offered a one-year foundation course in the language before her degree started.

This really was an amazing turnaround for Emily. She was excited and felt energised again. Her plan took the fear out of her exams and she coped with them much more easily as a result. This wasn't an excuse for Emily to go easy on her studies, but she did have a feasible and rather more exciting adventure as a backup plan. Emily did end up studying in Denmark and is currently in her final year at vet school doing brilliantly.

What's worrying you at the moment? Get organised and stop the panic. If everything went wrong tomorrow, what would you do? Listen to your intuition. What would need to change? What other options do you have? There is always a different way around things if you ask yourself the right questions and trust that your intuition will steer you in the right direction. Be calm, be focused, keep your contingency plan to hand and everything may just work out all right in the end.

Fairy godmothers really do exist

Trying to lose weight but finding it hard to stick to your goals? Are you always feeling disappointed because it takes only one sinful mouthful of gooey sticky pudding for all your best intentions to go right out of the window? Whatever goals you're fed up of missing, have a think about this tip and you may find some inspirational help.

Diets! A swearword in any girl's dictionary. For most of my clients and friends, if we're not *on* one, we're *talking* about one, marvelling at how some of us can stick to them like glue, while others just have to *think* the word 'diet' and reach for the chocolate in a fit of blind panic.

For most of my clients, weight has been an issue at some point and some have spent their whole lives breaking promises to themselves about what they're going to eat each day. The women I've spoken to break them for any number of reasons, mostly because they're totally stressed and overloaded, with far too much for just one brain and one pair of hands to cope with. With such enormously high targets to reach on a daily basis, it's no wonder it takes one moment of weakness for all our good intentions to come tumbling down, together with our promises, our pride and our pedestals!

During my career as a coach, I have discovered two common denominators when my clients find it hard to lose weight. First, they've never had a good enough reason to diet and, second, they've all been trying to do it on their own. In my view, two things need to happen when you decide to lose weight: there must be a really great and very exciting reason to do it and you must have a fairy godmother to help you. The fairy godmother idea, by the way, is not mine: she was born when I spoke to Kerry very early one morning.

Kerry has spent years losing weight, putting it back on, feeling awful about herself one month, elated the next. She was determined not only to get a grip on her weight issue but also to sort out and finally lay to rest the emotional turmoil that went with it. When I asked her why she wanted to lose weight, she told me she had an amazing reason. She had had a secret desire for most of her life to learn the guitar and perform her own songs live on stage.

Now, for most of us, the kinds of desires that involve hairbrushes, mirrors and air guitars are usually best kept a secret but in Kerry's case her secret desire had backup. She is musically talented, has a fantastic voice and has a mountain of songs that she has written and kept to herself. Kerry's goal was realistic and achievable and it was time to work out exactly what her goal meant to her. Part One of this new chapter in her life was to visualise and write down exactly how it was going to feel when she was on stage performing her own songs in public. This was to be Kerry's reason why she would lose weight.

I asked Kerry to see herself doing this in as much detail as she possibly could. When you have a goal, you have to make it become real in your mind. You have to become so familiar with it, you'll feel as if you'd seen it on television, as if it had already happened. It's imperative to imagine what people are saying to you, what you are wearing, where you are and who is there with you. All of these descriptions help your subconscious mind develop a picture for you to work towards, and that's exactly what Part One of this strategy is about: getting that picture in place to create a solid reason why you should lose weight.

When Kerry had her vision firmly ingrained in her mind, she told me she saw herself sitting on a tall stool in the middle of a small stage in a pub, surrounded by family and friends, singing her song to rapturous applause. She saw herself wearing brown cowboy boots, a Gypsy-style denim skirt, a gorgeous brown belt and a pretty vest top in green satiny material. She confided that those were the clothes she would love to wear but had never had the confidence to try. Now she made up her mind that these were the clothes she would wear for her debut performance.

'So,' I asked, 'now we have Part One of your grand plan, what's the obstacle where your diet is concerned? What is it that stops you from eating healthily?' 'Dinner out with my mum!' she giggled. Kerry has a great relationship with her mother and every weekend they go out to eat together, Kerry thinks, Oh what the hell! and orders anything she fancies from the menu – and of course it's always the stuff that dieters' nightmares are made of. So we needed to get her some help.

'When you're sitting there with the waiter on one side and your mum on the other, when it's most difficult to avoid temptation, what would make it easier?' I asked.

'I'd need a fairy godmother!' she exclaimed.

'OK,' replied a surprised and intrigued life coach, 'tell me about her.'

'Well she's very glamorous! She's tiny and silver with gold sparks coming off her. She's very pretty with cute fluttery wings and she's holding out a box of clothes for me. The box is huge. It's from one of those really expensive shops where they wrap everything very carefully in beautiful tissue paper. Inside are the clothes that I want to wear on my debut night, and she's whispering, "Do you want them or don't you?" '

The answer as you can imagine, was a great big 'yes'. So this was it: Kerry's action plan for saying no at the right time was a fluttery fairy godmother with gold sparks flying off her, holding a box of carefully wrapped clothes. Kerry was absolutely convinced that, whatever delicious dishes were on the menu, they could never give her the feeling that standing on stage in her new outfit promised.

If you had a fairy godmother, what would she look like? Which promises would she help you to keep? It doesn't have to be a food thing: it could be that you're spending too much, you never leave work on time, you don't drink enough water or you have real difficulty hauling yourself to the gym on those cold inhospitable nights. Which promises are you totally and utterly fed up with not keeping? Forget willpower. Give yourself a damn good reason to carry out your promises and then give yourself your very own fairy godmother to watch over you and remind you of your intentions. Stranger things have happened, and, if you're up for trying anything once, then take a chance on that fairy godmother of yours!

Terms and conditions

Did you read the small print of the terms and conditions before you got married? Do you ever feel that you wouldn't have signed up if you'd known it was going to be like this? Perhaps you didn't know marriage even came with terms and conditions. Well it does, and I'm not talking about the 'obey' thing. If you haven't got a copy, start writing one today.

At the start of most relationships, you and all the other things in your life are not only rosy: they're positively glowing! He appreciates you for who you are; you would never try to change him; you love him exactly as he is and just cannot fathom those 'relationship control freak' types who moan about the habits of their partners all the time. He brings you flowers, sends cute text messages and is a fantastic cook as well as being the best lover you've ever had. Not only that, he'd travel the length and breadth of the country if you asked him because his sensitive and caring nature just wants you to be happy. Feeling icky yet?

We've all been there and it's great. He's fantastic and the world is smiling. In the blink of an eye, though, the shine has worn off that sparkly engagement ring, the fab sexy underwear is looking a bit dingy, his culinary skills seem to have seeped out of his body with time – and as for the bedroom … er, well, let's just leave it at his culinary skills! The honeymoon period doesn't last for ever. Both of you are probably under a great deal of pressure at work. Perhaps you've fallen into the depths of domestic disharmony and now all you seem to talk about between the sheets is whether he's remembered to put the rubbish out, and could he kindly remember to flush the loo next time?

This isn't what we signed up for and, if we'd known life would turn out like this, would we make the same decision again? Relationships need to be cared for, nurtured and given space, time and energy. When the fun goes, it needs to be purposely reinjected into our lives – and that's where your terms and conditions come in.

Tracey hit the nail on the head one day when she said that not only should men come with an instruction manual but that marriage and long-term relationships should also come with terms and conditions. She and her husband live with terms and conditions and they work like this. When they got together, both of them sat down and came up with the ten things that they considered would mean they had a marriage to die for. They talked about what he would need to do to make her feel special and what she would need to do to make him feel like the most important man in the world. Most couples eventually stumble across this type of information but it's generally never voiced or written down, and doing this exercise makes the whole process a lot more purposeful and definite.

Terms and conditions are an informal agreement between the two of you, a code of conduct to live by and a safeguard for that time when the dizzy heights of the honeymoon period have definitely worn off.

Julia used this really well when she and her husband of fifteen years were bickering. Tensions were running very high in their household. They were shouting at each other constantly, arguing over money, and Julia spent a lot of her time alone and in tears. Julia told me they loved each other enormously and couldn't really think about being apart – it wasn't an option either one of them really wanted to consider, but they knew that staying together was making both of them miserable. How had it come to this? They had promised they would never fall into the trap of domestic dreariness, and that was exactly where they had ended up.

Neither had realised they'd fallen into it until a major argument had broken out. I spoke individually to Julia and John about their relationship, and it was clear that they adored each other but had no idea where to start making positive and lasting changes.

I asked them to imagine they had the perfect relationship. I asked them what they classed as a solid, happy and loving team and to picture themselves this time next year, having just had the best year ever, deeper in love than ever before, feeling like the most bonded couple in the history of the universe. What did they do on a daily basis? What kinds of things did they say to each other? How did they live? What did they look like? Where did they go? This was a relationship fantasy land where anything could happen. By taking the reality and negativity out of a situation, they were both able to build up a picture of unadulterated bliss.

Hardly realistic, though, I hear you scream. We can all wander off into the realms of fantasy where dirty dishes, morning breath and fake orgasms don't exist. You're right. This is the real world as we are all too often reminded, so we have to figure a way to blend uninterrupted bliss with stark reality!

In a perfect world, Julia's biggest wish to help turn her marriage from a war zone into a relaxing haven of indulgence was that her husband cook for her at the weekends. John is a great cook. He used his culinary finesse to woo her in the first place and she really missed the pampering of his weekend culinary masterpieces. Julia confided that resentment had probably been building up for years and, as a consequence, her frustration was blowing everything else out of proportion.

In John's dream world, Julia would praise him more often. This, he told me, wasn't just to massage his male ego but simply to make him feel he was getting it right sometimes and that his contribution was valued and appreciated. The joint condition they agreed on that day was that any discussions over money or bills would be done out of the house in their favourite coffee shop. This would help stop their home feeling like a war zone and meant that tempers would not flare in a public place.

Julia and John had their first terms and conditions and decided to live with them for the next month. I loved the day they came back to see me. All I need to tell you is that they were holding hands and smiling. Romance had been rekindled!

What is your relationship like and has it seen better days? Is it make-or-break time? Before you make any major life-changing decisions, show your other half this tip and come up with a few terms and conditions of your own. What would make you feel valued and appreciated? How could you turn yourself into the best partner in the world and what would you need to do differently? Life could be a whole lot happier with a few terms and conditions.

Your fifties are your twenties – with style!

Are you finding it difficult to come to terms with your age? Does the year you were born sound like centuries ago instead of decades? Do you cringe every time someone mentions your birthday? Then today's the day to turn your thinking around, stand up, be proud of your age and who you are.

About two years ago, I spoke to a lady who introduced herself as a managing director of a London company with a staff of twenty, 'Most of them probably wish I'd retire!' she joked. Proudly she told me she was 79! She never told me her name – it was a brief conversation – but I'll never forget her spirit and energy. Imagine, being 79 and still running your own company. Age clearly wasn't an issue for her – but it's a massive issue for some.

Why is it that we're all so age-conscious? Why do we match ability against age and assume that the older we get the further downhill we'll slide? We live in a time when everything seems age-related, so it's hardly surprising that we find it so hard to celebrate our experience, revel in our maturity and show off our years.

Forget your birth certificate! I'm much more concerned with who you are, what you've achieved and what you'd love to achieve next. As I've got older, I've noticed that friends and clients who view their ages positively look younger, feel younger and act younger than their natural years. They live their lives with smiles on their faces and a carefree attitude. They always have a thrilling story to tell and generally live with excitement and passion.

Who on earth said that, just because you hit fifty, your sense of style, your looks, personality and sense of fun and adventure have to go? I know several people in their fifties and older who look amazingly glamorous and elegant. One of my friends, Meg, took up running in her fifties and recently completed the Great North Run, something most *twenty*-year-olds wouldn't be fit enough to do!

Why should a number on your birth certificate dictate how enthusiastic you are for your life today? We don't have our ages lit up in neon signs above our heads, so the only way people guess our age is by the way we look, the way we dress and the way we behave. There's no rule book that says you have to behave a certain way once midnight strikes on a certain day of a certain year. If you can look in the mirror and honestly decide that you look older than your years, then choose to change today. Whom would you love to look like? How old would you love other people to think you are? How did you think you'd look when you got older, and is this it? Are you looking at her now? Not only that, are you ageist yourself? Do you make detrimental remarks about your age or other people's ages? Well, from today, know that your attitude could also be hindering your age. It's time to stop that clock.

It seems mad that when you're a child you wish the years away, only to want them back when you're older. We all know that physically we can't turn back time, and, if we could, would we really yearn for adolescence again? The thing is, not one of us has ever been our age before; this is the oldest we've been so far; this is the most experienced we've been yet. Consider this. You have managed to get as old as you have, yet millions of people all over the world were never lucky enough to reach your age, but *you* did. What have you lived through? What is the thing you're most proud of? What your chronicle age gives you is experience and it's that experience that you can offer others. It's important to be proud of your age and it's important that you tell people what you've achieved, otherwise they'll never know.

Another friend of mine, also called Meg, recently told me that she finds it totally inconceivable that she has actually reached the incredible age of fifty. Mentally, she still feels the same as she did in her twenties, yet she's raised four intelligent, clever and well-rounded children, enjoys a re-warding career as a complementary-health therapist and life coach, constantly inspires the people around her, including me, and makes time to explore a writing and presenting career in the process. Her experience makes her more valuable than she's ever been and her value only increases, the older she gets.

I'd been coaching Sylvie for several weeks before her hand leaped to her mouth in alarm one day as she realised that she'd just let slip her age. She confided that she was so ashamed of it that she'd actually made a secret pact with herself never to let on how old she really was. Sylvie explained that, since her last birthday, she had felt physically older. Suddenly, policemen were looking like children and she realised she preferred the radio stations that talked more to pop music channels. She realised, to her horror, she was becoming intolerant of youngsters and frequently started sentences with 'In my day …' or 'Years ago …' and still insisted on referring to old money when comparing today's soaring prices. Light-hearted and jovial as Sylvie's description of 'being old' was, the issue itself was actually quite serious and she hadn't realised how much her attitude towards her age was clouding her daily life. She felt low for much of the time and pegged her happiness on the day the scientists would produce the magic turn-the-clock-back drug.

I asked Sylvie to tell me the most amazing thing she'd ever done. I asked her what she had learned about herself, what she had taught others and how she had developed and grown as a person. The whole time she was talking, she was smiling, recounting various stories of how successful she'd been, the people she'd met, the times she'd been thanked for her vision and skill. I asked her what she would like to do next. She reeled off a whole list of things that she hadn't yet achieved, places she'd never been and experiences that she'd never got round to. That session inspired Sylvie to be proud of her age and who she'd turned into, and it was also the session that motivated her into planning more adventures for her future.

What have you achieved in your life? What valuable lessons have you learned about life and about yourself? Be proud of your experience and your value – they only increase with time.

Creating more time for busy women

How many times a day do you wish you had more time? Are you constantly working against the clock – and losing? Then you need to read this tip.

Do you find yourself wishing you had a magic wand that would just make everything in the world stop except you? Wouldn't it be great if everything and everyone came to a complete and silent standstill? Just one hour might be long enough for you to get yourself back on track and catch up with life, then you could press the start button and the world need never know what just happened. We're on a constant merry-go-round of engagements, pressures, appointments and promises – so how can you possibly make more time just appear from nowhere?

I couldn't help being reminded what a cheapskate I'd been back in 2004 when I'd bought my new A4 day-to-a-page diary from a pound shop. I'm an old-fashioned type of girl and can't be doing with anything computerised to run my life – I like my trusty pen and paper. That year, though, it seemed that I wouldn't be working on Tuesday the fourteenth and Wednesday the fifteenth of December, because those pages were missing. I know – it's no wonder it was only a quid!

Just as I was considering how resourceful I was being by writing out two little yellow stickies to add in the days, I stopped myself with one of those 'Aha!' moments. The penny had dropped: I had just thought of the most cunning plan ever. If those days didn't exist (well, in Lynette World, anyway), then I supposed I didn't have to work on them. A crafty smile was slowly broadening across my face when I realised that I could actually buy myself two whole days off to do whatever I liked. I could catch up on the never-ending stream of post and emails in my office; I could do the pile of hand washing that had accumulated since my holiday (yes, I was behind with the laundry!); I could take my dogs down to the beach for a run; or I could even just do nothing – spend the day in my pyjamas and watch films all day.

A few years ago my friend Liz's husband, Alan, stole her diary to do just that, tear pages out, so Liz would be forced to take a couple of well-earned days' rest during her pregnancy!

Self-indulgent? Inspirationally brilliant? Devilishly child-ish or deliciously wicked? Call it what you will, but I decided to surprise myself the following year with two days off somewhere in the year. I have ripped out two random days somewhere during the year when I'll least expect them. Imagine the delight of coming across two whole days knowing that you have no plans and no commitments – just pure unadulterated time with which to do whatever you wish!

This can work with families and children, too. Taking the odd day out of the family diary means that they can't schedule anything in, either, and you'll have the whole weekend to spend together exactly as you'd wish.

So that's exactly what Amelia decided to do after her coaching session. Amelia and her partner Paul have two young children. Amelia works part-time and looks after the children while her partner works full-time. They both enjoy busy and full lives, which means that quality time spent as a family is precious. The weekends are when Amelia would love to have her family around her more just to spend time together. The problem is that the week-ends are their busiest times. Amelia catches up on the housework, takes the children shopping, drops them off at various out-of-school activities, and her partner plays football every Sunday. Consequently, weekends are far from relaxing and they never spend any time together.

Amelia decided to put this tip into practice and tore the weekend pages out of the family diary, just a few weeks later. She didn't tell her partner; in fact, he didn't even notice until the Saturday morning. The children had no plans, she had no plans and, funnily enough, her partner had no plans, either.

After everyone had got over the shock, they planned their day, did exactly what they'd been speaking about for ages, and went to the zoo. This precious time meant the family could enjoy spending time in each other's company. Her husband was totally relaxed; the children were in bed exhausted by eight o'clock; and Amelia and Paul spent the rest of the evening watching a film together with a bottle of wine.

It is entirely possible to feel completely different after taking a day out of your usual routine. If day-to-day stress causes you to feel down, go shopping and spend too much, use this tip to take yourself out of the picture for a while. A bit of distance and a day off gives you a fresh perspective on problems and means that, when you go back, you're able to deal with them more positively.

If you need a reason to take a couple of days off, if stress is getting the better of you and you're running around on empty, or if you're self-employed and never find time to catch up on yourself, go on, dare yourself to rip a couple of pages out of next year's diary – and you might just find you have no choice!

Social butterflies and boyfriends

Finding yourself on an endless treadmill of work, home, sleep; work, home, sleep? Wishing for someone to share your life with? Longing for a social life but have no time to meet anyone? Then it's time to get what you really want and stop pretending.

For some people, being single is their worst nightmare. It seems that some of us crave society so much that we'll do anything not to spend time on our own, and, if we don't have a special someone to spend our time with, then we'd just rather be working. I've done it too. At one point, I was absolutely convinced that working all the time and being busy would make me seem more attractive or interesting. After all, being able to say, 'Oh, I can't do that day, but I can see you two weeks on Tuesday' sounds so much better than 'any evening this week'.

Whatever the reason, for some singletons, being busy is their excuse for 'not having time for a boyfriend'. Now I'm not claiming that every single person is desperate for their life's soul partner to come along. Indeed some people are far happier with their own company, suiting themselves and having a ball on the single scene. But, if you're reading this and that isn't you, then let me let you into a little secret: *working hard and filling your time won't get you a date*. In fact, it's important to realise that it's OK to have space in your diary and that it's beneficial to have some quality 'you time' when you're single.

It's very easy to get trapped in the mindset that 'busy' equals 'interesting', but I've got news for you: it doesn't. 'Busy' equals 'knackered'. You'll be tired, stressed and completely humourless with exhaustion. The endless work/sleep treadmill really isn't any fun. No sooner have you fought your way home through heavy traffic and unreliable public transport than you're starving hungry and end up bunging something congealed and prepacked in the oven before you crash in front of the television unable to string a sentence together (let alone muster up the energy to dress up and go out with friends).

If you've got a second job, you'll no doubt just have time to change your clothes and reapply your lippy before running out of the house again so you're not late and, if that's you, then television is a luxury. Let's face it, reading this book is a luxury, so well done if you've managed that bit! If you're working just so you don't have to go home and be on your own, if it's the only way you get a social life and you go to work just to be around people, if you've convinced yourself that any company is better than no company, I beg to differ.

We're all busy these days but, if you're on the lookout for love, being busy doesn't come across as sexy, inviting or intriguing. Any prospective date will assume that you're too busy to fit them in or that you're obviously too important and high up the career ladder to want a boyfriend and – dare I say it? – a family in the future. People pick up on what you put out there. The other part of this theory is that, if you've never really spent any time on your own, you won't know who you really are. Then, when you do go out on a date, what will you talk about? The job you do? The ins and outs of your office politics? That's likely to bore any date to death and you won't be showing him who you really are. Come to think of it, do you really *know* who you are? If the answer is no, then find out, and the way to do that is by spending some time in your own company – not working, not socialising, but learning to be happy entertaining yourself, finding out what makes you tick, having some quality 'you time', so you know who 'you' are.

Sally made massive progress between one coaching session and the next just one month later. She spoke to me about how lonely she was feeling. She said that her so-called friends never called her and, when she called them, they were always too busy to come to the phone or stop for a chat. Her social life was zero, she hadn't had a boyfriend in six years and her family lived miles away.

'So how does your day look?' I asked.

Sally explained she had two jobs: a new and demanding day job and then six or seven evenings a week. She rushed straight home to change before starting her evening job in a theatre. She told me how much she loved her theatre job. She even got really cheap tickets to see shows, but she had no friends to take with her. I pointed out to Sally what I assumed would be the glaringly obvious bit: all she ever did was work. Sally never knew whether her friends had phoned because she was never at home to answer the phone. Perhaps they used to phone her but got bored of trying when they could never get hold of her.

Sally told everyone she was always working so maybe they'd unwittingly dropped her from their social circle, assuming she'd be too busy to accept their invitations. Sally hadn't thought about any of those possibilities.

'What would you do with your time if you didn't work?' I asked.

She reeled off a whole list of things: she'd write poetry; she'd love to relax more; she was tearful and stressed (probably through tiredness) and she hadn't even read a book in ages (one of her favourite ways to destress). Sally agreed that financially she could afford to let some of her evenings at the theatre go, so she decided to cut her work-load down and have some time in her diary left totally clear. For what? Whatever came up. That's the point of keeping some space free in your diary, so you have some freedom to move should anything come up that you'd love to do.

The next time I spoke to Sally her situation had changed dramatically and she was bubbling with enthusiasm about what she'd been doing. I felt as if I were speaking to a different person altogether. She'd cut down her evenings at the theatre; she'd been away with a friend for a week; her social life had picked up and she was out all the time, not working but with friends; and she'd got herself a new boyfriend.

You have to take the brave step to make space in your diary and then let all your friends know you're available. They're not mind readers and, if you want a social life, you have to make the first move, so *stop working so hard*.

If Sally sounds a bit like you, and you're using work as an excuse not to have a social life, grab a pen, answer the questions below, and this could be your first step towards building a brand new social life.

What does your day currently look like?

_____

_____

_____

What would you like to do with 'free' time if you had any?

_____

_____

_____

Who would you like to spend more time with?

_____

_____

_____

What new hobbies would you love to take up?

_____

_____

_____

When do you plan to start creating some free time?

_____

Which friendships would you love to revamp?

_____

How would you ideally love to spend more 'you time'?

_____

What portion of your free time do you need to allocate just to you?

_____

Once you've answered these questions, let your friends know that you're going to be around more and that you've neglected them for far too long.

The tip is simple: work less; don't be in such a panic to fill time; dare to have unscheduled space in your diary; dare to spend some of that precious time of yours alone and learn how to be with yourself. The free time you build in will create room and space for old friends to reach you again and a few new friends to find you too.

Spiders and candles

Does the slightest negative comment from a well-meaning friend shatter your confidence? Are you someone who loses heart quickly when plans aren't coming together? Then light up your confidence with a candle and watch what happens.

Whenever I pick up the phone to a client, I have no idea what we will talk about. In fact, I make a point of not trying to anticipate the direction in which any coaching session will go. Sometimes, my clients pick up the phone and say, 'I know I should have my coaching session today but I've no idea what I'm going to talk about.' Within minutes, though, we are off on some subject or other, sometimes deep and meaningful, sometimes plotting sneaky ways of getting the children to listen to them at eight o'clock on a Monday morning when the household is at its most chaotic. When I picked up the phone to speak to Kerry, I never expected to talk about spiders and candles in the same sentence.

Kerry introduced herself to me as someone who gets very easily excited. She told me she had these amazing plans for herself: to write a book, to become a respected singer/songwriter and to run a marathon. These were just a few of her ideas, but she never seemed to be able to get any of them off the ground. No sooner would she start one project than she'd think of another two things to add to the list. Before she knew it, she was juggling ten ideas, and it might take only one person to say something negative before it all got too much and Kerry had given up, confident in the knowledge that her prediction had been fulfilled – that she couldn't achieve anything. She would kick herself for never being able to put anything into practice. Her confidence would disappear and she would end up feeling awful.

'It seems to me', I said, 'that you've got all these legs you want to grow and haven't got a big enough body to attach them all to.' Kerry agreed and said she felt like a spider with a very small body and too many legs! I suggested that, rather than work with her on one of her many projects, we try first to grow her body a bit. Her body, in this instance, was a metaphorical term for her self-confidence, her inner strength. Kerry told me that this was very weak. Every time she 'failed' at something, every time someone said something negative to her, she would end up feeling like a naughty four-year-old who's about to be found out. This affected her work life and her personal life. Kerry often put up a very strong, competent, independent and outgoing front, but inside she felt as if she were faking it.

My aim was to help Kerry grow a sturdy and strong inner self. That way, whenever someone knocked her self-esteem with a negative comment, they wouldn't be able to push her over; she would have the inner strength and confidence to stand firm in the knowledge of her abilities. I felt sure that, once she felt stronger about herself, she would feel much more in control of the projects she wanted to complete and stand a better chance of being able to pull them *all* off.

Here's where the candle comes in. I asked Kerry to close her eyes for a moment and visualise a candle with a glowing flame in the middle of her chest. I was completely silent for thirty seconds while Kerry visualised her candle. She described it to me as a very small flame wafting around in the breeze, probably about to go out. I then asked her to visualise it for another thirty seconds, but this time I asked her to try to grow it. Kerry was able to grow her candle so much that she physically felt the warm glow of the flame across her whole body and up to her chin. Part of Kerry's homework that week was to continue growing her flame. I asked her to concentrate on her candle every time she felt 'wobbly'. It was to be Kerry's reminder of the strong, confident person she was on the inside. In times of insecurity, her candle would no longer look as if it were about to go out. Instead, she would visualise it as being tall, strong and bright. It has worked brilliantly. Kerry's candle now holds a brilliantly strong flame that covers the whole of her upper body and she feels very much in control.

Since Kerry started to increase her inner strength with her candle, she is a changed woman. Not only has she started a running programme and entered herself into the next London Marathon, but she has written, sung, recorded and produced her own song on CD, is learning to play the guitar (a childhood dream), has lost two stone in weight because of the exercise and has got a fantastic new man – all this, as well as being the managing director of her own company. She is taking each of her dream projects and laying down firm and solid plans for bringing them to life.

What does your candle look like? How could you use Kerry's story to inspire and influence yourself? She is proof that, if you believe in yourself and feel strong inside, you can do anything you put your mind to.

If you feel your inner strength and sturdiness is an issue, take a minute to visualise what it actually looks like. From now on, grow your inner candle and rely on it to keep you strong when you need it most, and you'll feel able to challenge the world.

Positive potential

Would you love to boost the confidence of those around you but don't know how? Are you desperate to let someone you love know how much potential they really have? Then read this tip – suitable for use on ages one to one hundred.

I speak to a lot of women who would love to have more confidence, but I also speak to women who would love nothing more than to be able to boost the confidence of other people in their lives. Isn't it so frustrating when you see potential in someone and, no matter how much you praise them, promote them and encourage them, they just can't see that potential themselves? The basic rule is, if they don't believe they have potential, if they don't believe in themselves, they won't be able to achieve their true potential, because it is only ever as high as we believe it to be. If you live or work with someone who could be making much more of themselves, if you'd love to learn how to bring that person out and build up their confidence, this will help.

I was recently invited to attend a coaching weekend hosted by the Life Coaching Academy and I sat in on one of Nic Rixon's sessions. Nic Rixon is one of the most energetic and enthusiastic people I have had the pleasure of knowing and, in his talk, he explained that he never puts anyone down, he never, ever criticises anyone. If you're wondering how you can possibly go through life without ever criticising anyone, this is how.

It's what Nic calls 'evidence-based feedback'. In order to boost someone's confidence, you need to give them firm evidence that they're good at something – positive feedback must always come first. You need to tell them exactly what they're doing that means they're a success before you go in with the compliment, otherwise it's just empty flattery. For instance, if you say to someone, 'You're great at sales', they won't necessarily believe you. However, it would be different if you backed it up by saying something like, 'I saw the way you made that customer laugh. You built up a great rapport within seconds, which is why he bought the more expensive shirt. That shows off your great sense of humour and that's how I know you're an excellent salesman'. Now that's more credible, isn't it?

Imagine for a second how it would feel to go through life never, ever being put down by anyone and always having your special strengths pointed out. Imagine going to work every day and never being humiliated by someone broad-casting your mistakes. Imagine what living in that kind of relaxed and positive environment might do to your self-image, your self-confidence, your view of your own poten-tial. How would it feel if no one ever said anything derogatory about you or to you? It's an interesting concept, and if we used this tactic all the time it would be considered a way of life. It would be taken for granted, and that would be quite cool, wouldn't it?

Think back to your childhood for a minute. Who sticks in your mind? What comments do you remember being made about you in the past? Think back to your school days. Do you remember a particular teacher or a class-mate, perhaps? The chances are that you remember them because (a) they put you down or (b) they built you up! Unfortunately, the chances are (because our subconscious minds tend to work this way) that you remember the putdown and the fact that they told you that you were useless at something – and that's not a great feeling at all.

Now imagine how you might feel if someone else remembered you for having put them down. Imagine that someone, somewhere, is reading this same paragraph and remembering you because you once told them they were stupid or useless. How uncomfortable would it be to know that you might have hindered someone else's development, crushed their confidence or stopped them achieving their potential by a careless remark you made long ago? That's not a pleasant thought, either. This tip may not make particularly comfortable reading but I guess we've probably all put somebody down in the past, and we may not even have been aware of it. You can do something about it from today though, and you can make sure that you're never again remembered for making someone feel bad about themselves.

Make two promises to yourself right now:

1. never to put anyone down again;

2. practise 'evidence-based feedback'.

If you're a manager or in a position of authority, tell your staff what strengths they have and what specifically they do to show off those strengths. When you next talk to someone, listen to what they're saying and come up with at least five strengths that person possesses, then tell them exactly where and when they use those strengths. Try it on your peers at work, try it on your children. Try it for a week and see what kind of reaction you get.

This is major attitude-changing stuff and something we could all do with thinking about more often. After all, why exactly are you telling someone how badly they've done? We'd all like to think we don't get pleasure from pointing out someone's mistakes; we'd all like to think that we don't do it to boost our own egos. The reasons we put others down *are our own*, they generally have everything to do with our own insecurities and low self-esteem and very little to do with someone else's development. If this sounds like you, stop doing it today and see what a difference it makes.

It's a girl thing

If the word 'diet' brings you out in a cold sweat, if the phrase 'forbidden foods' sends a shiver down your spine, if thoughts about eating consume you from dawn till dusk, here's an idea to change your attitude.

Why is it that some people eat junk food all day without putting on an ounce of weight, while others just have to look at a pork pie and the thought of that bikini goes right out of the window? Food is something we can't do without and, with slimming magazines galore, no one can be excused for not knowing the calorie difference between a bar of chocolate and an apple. It's everywhere we look. Obesity is one of the British government's biggest concerns, but have you ever considered that obesity isn't just about the food we eat? It could be our attitude to diets that's the key issue here and could be more to do with the diet-versus-healthy-eating school of thought.

I saw Debbie when she was feeling particularly low about her weight and her eating habits. She told me that when she's on a diet she feels fantastic, she loses weight, feels happier about herself, looks better and has tons of energy. The problem is that it takes just one sinful bar of chocolate and the whole thing goes to pot, leaving her feeling so guilty and bad about herself that she doesn't even want to go out. She gives up completely and any weight she has lost gets piled straight back on, together with a little extra.

I asked Debbie to tell me the difference between what she eats when she's on a 'diet' and what she eats when she gives up. Her 'diet' is full of vegetables, salads, fruit, fresh lean meat and fish with plenty of water, and she forbids herself things such as chocolate, biscuits, cake, sugar, pasta, coffee and tea. Alarm bells started to ring for me at the word 'forbid'! It was no surprise that, when she fails to keep up her strict diet, she ends up feeling bad about herself. When that happens, she starts eating processed food, fast food, takeaways and chips.

I asked Debbie what would happen if she allowed herself the healthy 'diet' *and* the occasional chocolate bar with some tea/coffee throughout the day if she felt like it. What if she filled up on the fresh food first and then allowed herself the occasional treat afterwards? She told me that it wouldn't be a diet at all.

'What would it be?' was my next question.

'Really easy!' she said.

The penny had dropped. I asked Debbie to see the food she ate not as a strict diet but as a healthy-eating plan in general. I explained that, to my mind, when she was on a so-called 'diet', what she was describing was actually a sensible eating plan and that it wouldn't be unreasonable for her to add the odd chocolate bar. It didn't mean she was a failure or that the whole thing had gone to pot.

It doesn't take a nutritionist to work out that the more weight you want to shift, the fewer fatty foods you should consume and the more exercise you need to take. But in this case Debbie had been setting such strict targets for herself that she was doomed to failure from the start. Once she agreed to concentrate on eating healthily *in general*, she found it much easier to lose weight and keep it off without the guilt. In fact, now that she is filling up on healthy and plentiful dinners, she doesn't seem to crave the sweet stuff as much. Debbie no longer *forbids* herself food, and the weight is shifting. This is one diet that Debbie has no trouble sticking to.

Eradicate the words 'diet' and 'forbid' from your vocabulary today. Treat your body with respect, give it healthy, fresh food but, unless you have to for medical reasons, don't deny yourself the odd treat!

Energy conservation for busy women

Feeling tired all the time? Worried you don't have the energy to get everything done? This is a great strategy for protecting your energy and natural reserves.

This is a fantastic exercise for conserving your body's natural energy. First, if your energy is being zapped, you need to find out why, and it could be that you're not giving your body the proper fuel it needs in the form of food. It's important not to let your blood sugar levels get too low, and you can do that by eating three meals a day — healthy meals though, avoiding sugary drinks and chocolate. Breakfast is the most important meal of the day, and, after a whole night of fasting, sugar-coated cereal really isn't going to cut it, girls! Great as it tastes, our bodies can't always work with huge intakes of sugar and you can feel full, exhausted, bloated and very tired if your diet is generally unhealthy. Tiredness is also a symptom of dehydration, so make sure you really are drinking plenty of water throughout the day to keep your energy levels and general alertness high. Make sure you give yourself and your body time to relax properly. Do something for yourself at least once every week and make sure that you have fun for at least half an hour every day, because laughing is a fantastic tonic. If none of that helps though, don't bury your head in the sand: get yourself checked out by your GP or complementary-health therapist.

Whatever the reason, use this tip as a backup to keeping your energy reserves properly topped up. Don't be fooled – just because this is a backup, don't underestimate how powerful this exercise can be. It's helped many of my clients boost their energy levels and return to being in control of their hectic lives. Protect yourself and you'll breeze through the day ahead just that little bit more easily.

This can be done at any time when you feel your energy levels start to drop, but, if you don't remember to do it during the day, then think about it when you finally get to bed just before you drift off. Imagine that there is a light inside your body (maybe it's the candle from earlier in the book). Now imagine that there are tiny holes all around your body where the light is shining through. Your aim here is to keep all of the light in your body by plugging up the holes. The light represents your body's energy and your job is to go around all the holes one by one and mentally plug them up. Concentrate and visualise seeing each hole and gap close. You'll feel more powerful and energised as you do it. It need take only a few minutes, but make sure that you don't have any leaks! We demand a lot from ourselves physically and mentally, so help yourself by making sure you keep all of your energy inside.

Radiating gorgeousness!

Ever wanted to be the kind of woman who radiates gorgeousness? Ever secretly wanted heads to turn when you walk into a room? Maybe you'd love to render total strangers speechless with your beauty! Forget botox – get attitude. Here's how.

Gorgeousness isn't just a pretty outer skin: it's a way of feeling inside, and it's something that others around you pick up on, rather like an invisible aura. It comes from the inside and needn't come in the form of high heels and hot pants on a size-eight model!

Have you ever come across someone who literally glows in a room full of people, who oozes charm and sexiness from every pore? It doesn't matter what you look like, or what dress size you are. It is entirely possible for anyone to radiate gorgeousness. You just have to believe it.

Josie came to see me because she was dissatisfied not only with her life but also with herself. She told me at that very first meeting that she didn't like herself, she hated the way she looked, she avoided mirrors and looked away from her reflection in shop windows. Josie had been injured in a road traffic accident about twenty years before, and her face was disfigured as a result. She has a small group of friends with whom she feels confident and those friends know just how she has felt about her looks since her accident, right through her thirties and forties and now in her fifties. Even her marriage had collapsed because of her lack of confidence.

However, Josie's picture of herself seemed a far cry from the way her friends saw her, and no amount of reassuring her how gorgeous they thought she was and no amount of stylish clothes, treats or expensive accessories was going to cut it. She had to learn how to feel gorgeous from the inside, how to capture that special feeling and to bottle it, to use whenever she needed it.

I asked her how she thought gorgeous people felt. She said they'd probably feel confident, they'd laugh a lot, they'd have no problem walking into packed restaurants on their own, they'd have that something special about their personality that exuded warmth and confidence, something she was convinced she didn't have.

What I asked Josie to imagine next was particularly hard for her. I asked her to close her eyes and imagine that she was already gorgeous. I asked her to visualise how she would act in a room full of people. This was so far away from her comfort zone and she had spent so long feeling negative about her looks and lack of confidence that she had forgotten what it was like to feel really gorgeous. I asked her to practise feeling gorgeous when she was alone, in the privacy of her home when no one was watching.

When we spoke a week later, Josie had been practising diligently all week. She told me that, if she felt truly gorgeous, she wouldn't try to hide her scar, she would consider it part of her and her history and it would make her unique, interesting even. In a room full of people where she considered herself gorgeous, everyone would react differently to her and feel comfortable around her; they would genuinely want to talk to her. In her mind's eye, she'd be wearing perfume and a new dress; she'd be throwing her head back when she laughed and wouldn't avoid making eye contact with strangers. It seemed that Josie's scar would be almost invisible to her and, as a result, to everyone else.

She thought back to the time just after the accident, when her children were babies. They never questioned her scars; they didn't react to her differently when she came out of hospital. They simply looked into her eyes and saw their mum. She had forgotten that and thought that, if she made eye contact more often, maybe people would see her and not her scar.

I asked Josie to practise being gorgeous every day and to change one thing about her behaviour and way of thinking that would mean she was closer to her goal. She said she would wear perfume, something she hadn't done for years, and she would assume that people were looking at her and not her scar.

Three months into our coaching sessions, Josie had attended a friend's wedding. It had been a nerve-racking event for her, since most of the guests had not seen her since her twenties and they had never seen her scar. I was immensely proud at the way Josie tackled that day: she held her head high with pride, practised everything we had talked through and, later, she sent me this email:

> Lynette, the difference is massive, I feel completely different about myself, I never knew I could be this confident and the feeling is truly mind blowing.

If you felt totally mind-blowingly gorgeous, how would you behave? How would others treat you? What would be different about you? You've read a bit about how the way you think determines both your own behaviour and how other people respond to you. Make a list below of five things that you would choose to change about your behaviour or the way you think about yourself that would mean you felt drop-dead gorgeous.

1. _____

2. _____

3. _____

4. _____

5. _____

Choose one thing from that list and put it into practice today. Feeling beautiful isn't something that can be bought or given to you. Don't hang around waiting for others to make you feel good – you'll be waiting a lifetime. Instead, make yourself feel beautiful from the inside and turn your soul into pure gorgeousness.

Divine intervention

Do you believe in angels? Have you ever asked for something to happen and it's miraculously appeared as if from nowhere? Perhaps you're a total sceptic and believe that we're on our own in this life. Whatever your thoughts, sometimes a little divine intervention is called for ...

A couple of years ago, I was wandering around the shops, when I came across the most beautiful figurine of an angel. She was very simple, exquisitely made and just perfect as a present for my friend Barbara. The next time I saw her, I gave her the present and she burst into tears. It wasn't the angel that had made her cry but what it represented. Just days before, Barbara's daughter had gone through a dreadful crisis and had been badly hurt. As she was so desperately worried about her, the angel seemed the perfect gift, although I had no idea what had happened when I bought it. Even more extraordinary was that another friend of Barbara's had also given her an angel that very afternoon. How often do you receive not one but two angels in the same day? How come two of Barbara's friends had chosen to give her angels when she needed them most?

The whys and wherefores are not mine to answer. I don't have any of the answers, and I'm certainly no expert on angels. But what I do know is that I believe in them. I believe that, if you ask for help or reassurance, they can help you.

I was first introduced to the concept of angels by my great friend Julia. She taught me that, if you ask for help or guidance, they often give you signs to demonstrate that you are travelling in the right direction. She once described to me how, years before, she was heavily in debt and at crisis point. Julia asked her angel for a sign that everything in the greater picture was OK and that she was on the right path in life. The following day, a friend of hers called and asked her how much money she would need to clear her debts. 'More than I care to tell you!' she replied. Her friend had just been left a vast sum of money, much more than she needed, and had decided to pay off all of Julia's debts with part of her windfall. For Julia, that was the sign she needed that meant she was doing the right thing and was on the right path.

Now, for all you sceptics out there, this is not your perfect call to the divine to miraculously get all your debts paid off tomorrow. If it were, this tip might have appeared much earlier in this book! Yes, in Julia's case, her debts were cleared, but actually Julia hadn't asked for them to be cleared. What she had asked for was a sign that she was doing the right thing. That's the difference.

Asking angels for help isn't about profiting financially: it's about gaining a certain strength or trust in yourself that all will be fine. Even though we can't see the bigger picture, there will be a reason why we sometimes go through very desperate and sad periods of our lives. Maybe we're being taught something; maybe we'll come out stronger people. The point is that we don't know, so asking angels for help has more to do with clarity and internal peace of mind than profiting financially. It just so happened that Julia's call for help was answered in this way.

Another client, Michelle, came to see me when she was at a crossroads in her career. After realising that her current job held no great interest for her, she was torn between studying for two brand new careers. She considered what both options would give her, but had no idea how to make the choice. Michelle decided to ask her angel for guidance. 'Which option would help me continue with my true life's path?' she asked out loud, after her coaching session one day.

The following day, a friend called her with a very exciting proposition. Her friend had seen an opportunity for two work placements abroad and asked her if she would like to come with her. She knew immediately that this was the opportunity she'd been waiting for. That was three months ago (as I write this), and, although Michelle is quite often out of email or telephone contact, she emailed me just a week ago with news that she is thrilled with her new direction, and her new lifestyle gives her more satisfaction than she could ever have hoped for. Some might say this is coincidence, some might say it was fate. Whatever it is, the opportunity came only after she asked for help.

I've heard some people describe angels as people, everyday men and women who look like you and me but just seem to appear in an emergency or crisis. They offer valuable words of comfort and help when it's most needed. Other people are sure that their angels exist because they feel a calming presence and a sense of protection. On the other hand, I've also spoken to other people who claim to have seen their angels, know their names even, what they represent and how they work. Angels mean different things to different people and they are perceived completely differently by everyone. But ask anyone what their experience of angels is and they're likely to reel off a story of a friend of a friend who swears by their help.

Not everyone believes in angels though, and this tip is not about asking you to believe in something you don't: it is purely about having an open mind and trying something you may never have tried before. If you find yourself in a situation where you feel out of control, in need of help or guidance, or if you're having a particularly difficult time, this may just help to give you the answers or comfort you need. All it requires of you is that you ask the question and see what happens.

If you've never asked an angel for help before or never considered the possibility that angels exist, then you might not be entirely sure how to contact yours. There are mountains of books written by angel experts who will tell you exactly how to reach them. However, I can only tell you how I've used angels in the past. I just ask the question out loud, as if I were speaking to a real person, someone who perhaps knows a little more about the reasoning behind a situation than I do. Ask for reassurance, ask for a sign that all is well, and then keep your eyes and ears open.

Childlike charm

Do you find it difficult to make new friends? Do you get too shy to speak to strangers? This is the simplest strategy ever – even a child could do it.

Several years ago, I was wandering around a shop, when I caught the eye of a member of staff I thought I recognised. We smiled briefly in acknowledgement, but I had no idea where I thought I recognised her from or who she was.

I carried on looking around the shop, but we kept catching each other's eye until, in the end, she was brave enough to come up to me and say, 'I think I recognise you. Have we met before?' It was actually a huge relief that one of us had mustered up the courage to ask. We went through all the various places we had worked and spent time before finally we realised that she had been the manager of a well-known clothes shop that – shall we say? – I spent a lot of time in when I had my very first job. That was back in the days when all my earnings went on clothes! It was so long ago that the chain doesn't even exist now. We had never really spoken at the time, but there we stood in the shop, face to face after many years.

We got on really well, asking about each other's life, what we were doing and how our families were. We discovered we had a lot in common and chatted for ages. Then I paid for my purchases and left, without exchanging phone numbers. Occasionally, I'd go back to the shop and enjoy a chat if she was there, until one day we met in a car park and she said, 'Do you know, we often bump into each other and I think you're really nice. Would you like to be my friend?' No one had said that to me since school – *early* school! She told me her daughter was always coming home with new friends and that she just asked the girls at school if they'd like to be her friend. Rebecca thought it was such a shame that, as adults we never, ever say that, so she thought she would risk it, and we've been good friends ever since.

Isn't it daft that, when we become adults, it can be so difficult to forge new friendships? I know, sometimes it's just another job on the to-do list, one of those New Year resolutions – 'must make more friends this year'. It takes time to build up a new friendship though, and we often find it hard to keep in touch with the friends we already have. How many times have you had a brief conversation with someone and got on famously, only never to see them again? That person could have been really good to spend time with, to laugh with, to take up a new hobby with or meet for a coffee every so often. We never know what connections we'll make – and those connections get made only because one person plucks up the courage to say, 'Hi.' Perhaps we can learn a thing or two about how to make new friends from children.

Why is it that adults believe people would think us silly for asking others to be our friend? I loved the fact that Rebecca said that to me and have told many of my other friends and clients about it. During one of my sessions with Jennifer, she thought she could use a version of Rebecca's line.

Jennifer, by her own admission, is pretty bad at keeping in touch with people. Her job often demands that she work unsociable hours, so, when she does have a day off, her other friends are at work. She usually finds herself doing the shopping, catching up on the ironing, changing beds, picking the children up from school, and, before she knows it, it's dinner time, then bath time and she's exhausted. Jennifer told me how she'd love someone to have coffee with during the day or someone to go shopping with.

She also told me that she often put off going to new places, because she was so shy and found it hard to make new friends. She was aware that her shyness could come across as arrogance – but even that didn't make it any easier for her to make conversation. I asked her to pretend for a minute that she was really good at making new friends, that speaking to total strangers was a piece of cake and that she was going to a party where she would know no one. 'What would be your conversation opener?' I asked.

After Jennifer had finished shuddering at the thought, she said she'd probably find someone who looked approachable, smile, walk up to them and say, 'Hi, I don't know anyone here. I'm Jennifer. I thought you looked a nice person to say hello to!' Even for the most confident among us, being scared at a party is one of the most common issues, and Jennifer's opening line is one of the best I've heard. First of all, she's being honest by saying that she doesn't know anyone and, second, she's compli-menting the person she's meeting. I defy anyone not to be flattered by that introduction.

However, saying it in the confines of a coaching session and doing it in real life are worlds apart, but much to Jennifer's surprise, at a school PTA meeting later that week, she actually said it to one of the other parents. It turned out that they got on very well, their children were in the same class and they'd be meeting up the following week. This was a massive step for Jennifer and she probably took it only because she had an opening line prepared.

Don't be afraid to make new friends. The most honest and simple lines are often the most effective. Don't try to be someone you're not. If Jennifer's or Rebecca's opening lines sound like something you could imagine yourself saying, then remember them. If not, what would be your opening line? What would you feel comfortable saying? Maybe you fancy stealing a line from the questions in *Friends Re-connected*. What would you love someone to say to you at an awkward dinner party? Remember, honesty is the best policy, as is childlike charm.

Identity crisis

Do you feel as if you've reached a dodgy age and yearn to have your twenties back? Have you spent so long being a wife or a mum that you can't remember who you are any more? Then step back in time and bring the present back to life.

We've all heard of a midlife crisis. Some of you may even have had one, but have you ever had an identity crisis? Maybe you're having one right now and aren't even aware of it. It's little wonder that we go through periods when we question who we really are, when you consider *what* we are and to whom. If I were to ask you, 'Who are you?' what would you say? A wife? A mother? A housewife? A secretary? A managing director? We girls are many things to different people: we're best friends, we're daughters, we're colleagues, we're partners or wives, so you'd be easily forgiven for having an identity crisis occasionally.

Amanda is a housewife in her forties who gave up work after her first child was born. Her husband is the bread-winner and she lives in the country with her two children, who are now teenagers. Idyllic? Well, it looks that way on paper, but that wasn't how Amanda was feeling when she sought coaching. She told me she had been so caught up in looking after everyone else's needs, being a taxi service, housekeeper and general runaround, that she'd forgotten who she was, what kind of things she liked to do and even what her opinion was these days. When I asked who she was, she replied, 'A wife and a mother.'

Now there's nothing wrong with being a wife and a mother, but Amanda didn't feel able to introduce herself as 'Amanda' because she wasn't sure who Amanda was any more. It even occurred to her during that first session that nobody even called her Amanda these days. To her children, she was 'Mum' and to her husband, she was 'darling', which, endearing as it sounds, didn't make her feel valued or even noticed as a person in her own right.

I asked Amanda who she used to be before she got married. She explained that she'd met her husband at work, when she had enjoyed a well-respected career with a bank. Three years into their marriage, Amanda had fallen pregnant and she and her husband had decided that she should give up work to become a full-time mum, something she had always felt very strongly about.

Becoming a mother for the first time hadn't been as easy as she had imagined, though. She had felt totally swamped by the effect this little bundle had had on her life. He had turned everything she knew upside down and she remembers never quite feeling like herself again. Following the arrival of their much wanted second baby, the feeling that the old Amanda was lost for ever worsened as she saw herself very much as a wife and mother, putting herself second to the demands of her family.

When money had been tight, her husband and children always had the new clothes, while she had stopped having expensive haircuts in her old salon and even stopped colouring her hair, which had always been her trademark. Contact with her former colleagues had gradually dwindled over the years and she hadn't been to the gym since the day she left work. Amanda had hidden all of the old 'pre-children' photo albums, as she felt so far removed from the person she once was that it upset her too much to look at them.

'How on earth do I find out who I've turned into and, if I find her, what happens if I don't like her?' she said dispiritedly. Amanda felt as though she'd completely lost her identity, so we sat down and talked through a strategy to help her rediscover the old Amanda.

The first thing I asked her to do was to get out all her old 'pre-children' photos and have a good look at them. Painful as this was, Amanda needed reminding of the person she used to be if she was to reconnect with her old self. I asked her to remember when the photos were taken, where she had been, what she had been doing and whom she was with. We forget masses of things we have done in the past, and photos are the link as well as a memory jog. Amanda waited until both children were out and her husband was working late, then she put on some of her favourite music and climbed into the loft in search of the albums.

The next time I saw Amanda, she arrived with a long list of things she remembered doing, places she loved going and people she hadn't seen for years. She was shocked to see how much she had changed physically over the years and told me that she never thought she'd look like this. The old pictures became an incentive to get back the woman she had been and to start looking more like a grown-up version of the teenager she saw in the photos.

Money these days wasn't as tight as it had been in the past, so the very first thing she decided to do was visit a really luxurious and trendy salon in the town, because she'd decided to dye her hair back to the auburn it had been. Next, Amanda suggested to her husband that they visit their old haunts from the time when they first got married. They went away for the weekend, revisited the restaurants they had dated in and some of the art galleries they had spent hours wandering around. This was the start of Amanda's reconnecting with the woman she used to be, the woman she'd lost sight of and the woman her husband had fallen in love with.

Over a period of three months, instead of trying to forget her past, she made an effort to remember it: she called people she used to see; she remembered how she loved to read books in smart coffee bars; she was reminded in the photos of how well she used to dress. Gradually, she started to become the older person she had always imagined she would turn into. Yes, she was still a wife and a mother but now she felt closer to her younger self. She enrolled in evening classes to stimulate her mind and, as I write, she plans to do her MA, something she promised herself she'd do one day. Incidentally, her husband calls her by her name these days and her children have been taught to be a bit more self-sufficient in order to give Amanda more time to herself.

So, who are you? Are you the person you thought you'd grow into? What kinds of things made you 'you' ten, twenty years ago and are you still enjoying those things? If you're having an identity crisis, get back to basics. Remember a time when you felt life was exciting, when you felt interesting and alive. What clothes did you wear? What did you love doing? There's no need to get the hairspray out in an attempt to recreate the sixties beehive, and, whatever you do, forget those eighties skin-tight jeans. You've moved on, times have moved on, but bring back the fun, the love, the passion and the excitement of your former self and recreate your identity today.

Create a masterpiece!

Are you feeling trapped in a world of facts, figures and deadlines? Free your creative right brain and become a child again. Here's how.

I was thrilled when a client, Judith, surprised me with a painting when we met for one of our coaching sessions in London. Judith and I had been speaking about her love of art and life drawing and she had started going to art classes again both to find time for herself and to rekindle her passion for painting. Judith's picture is hanging in my office. I see it every morning when I walk in and every morning it always makes me smile.

Judith isn't the only client I have with a love for acrylic paint. Another client, Hannah, inspired her husband Tom to roll up his sleeves and get painting. Just days after trying to convince her that he couldn't paint to save his life, Tom's inspiration overtook him one day and he went in search of some old paint left over from the decorating in the garage. By the time Hannah came home, the finished masterpiece was drying in the middle of their lounge floor. She told me how she was led in blindfolded with strict instructions to stand on the sofa to get the 'full effect', before Tom proudly announced that she could open her eyes.

I've seen the painting and it is just amazing. He had painted a huge four-foot-by-five-foot canvas in orange and pink emulsion! The best bit about that painting, Hannah tells me, is the smile it brings to her husband's face every time she proudly tells someone that he's the artist. That's the point, you see: he painted it! My other point is that *everyone* can paint – without exception. You don't have to be Picasso or Turner, you don't have to go to night school, you don't have to have studied art or be brilliant at still-life drawing – in fact, you don't even need a steady hand or a paintbrush. All you need is a blank canvas (or big sheet of paper), a couple of leftover tester pots in colours you love and the courage to literally pour the paint onto the canvas, play with it with your hands and fingers, leave it to dry and then hang it on the wall. This is one of the fastest ways of letting your creative talents out! Being arty is a particularly right-brain thing. Right-brainers (people who predominantly use the right side of their brains) tend to be creative and dislike working with numbers, strict schedules, and constraints and limitations. Right-brainers prefer freedom, movement and fluidity in their lives.

However, the problem is, that we live in a predominantly left-brain world. Offices and schools throughout the land are constrained by targets, pressure, stress, getting facts and figures right and time scales – the kind of stuff that sends right-brainers mad. Life seems to revolve around left-brain activities and, whether you're a true left-brainer or not, it's imperative, in order to gain a sense of balance, that your creative side be set free from time to time and given permission to bubble to the surface. It's vital that your creativity not be stifled.

This tip is about how to use your right brain when you think you're the least right-brain person you know. It's about thinking that you're completely colour-blind and not at all artistic, and then getting the thrill of putting your work on the wall with the smug satisfaction of being able to tell intrigued visitors that you're the artist.

Here's my call to action for you – and I don't want to hear anyone scream that they can't paint. This is kids' stuff. You probably did it in play school and you probably did it throughout senior school. Get back in touch with your creative side (every single one of you has one) and get painting. Do a painting for your office, your bedroom, your lounge, your child's bedroom, the local hospital. Auction it for charity; give it to an old people's home; brighten up your workplace; brighten up your life; inject a bit of colour and passion and do something you've never done before.

Here are a few tips to get you started. You can buy canvases cheaply from art shops or even DIY shops. Buy a few different-coloured tester pots and roll up your sleeves. For a calm and serene painting, something that's going to make you feel relaxed in an insane world, smooth paint along the canvas with your hands, either vertically or horizontally (it'll look like a sunset in no time!), and, for a painting to excite and stimulate your senses, have some real fun: flick paint on to the canvas, get your cats to walk across it, get your two-year-old to help you and, lastly but most importantly, write your name at the bottom. Buy a canvas each for your whole family and make it a weekend paint-fest. You could sell them at car boot sales or on e-Bay; you could even set up your own business as a sideline. Emulsion tester pots are cheap and emulsion comes off with soap and water, so any mess will be easily cleared up. If this book teaches you nothing, let it teach you to be inspired and inspire others! Whatever you do this week, bring a smile to your face – go and paint!

Orgasmically high on life – naturally!

Can't seem to get excited about life any more? Can't remember the last time you felt so exhilarated about something, you nearly burst? The truth is, you could be numbing all your feelings in your bid to cope. Don't panic, though, for help is at hand. Take inspiration and read this.

Gillian had telephoned me for her first life coaching session, having just gone through a mammoth year by anyone's standards. This was Gillian's positive new start and, after taking the very brave decision to take her life by the scruff of the neck and hire me as her coach, all of a sudden she didn't quite know where to start.

Gillian felt exhausted most of the time. She was planning to start her master's degree in a few months but felt totally unprepared for the huge demand on her time and energy she knew it would bring. She, like many women, likes to pull things off to perfection. The worries and stresses she had gone through over the previous year, coupled with her need to be perfect in every area of her life, meant that she was filled with fear at the thought of her new challenge and hadn't got the first clue how she was going to fit everything in.

Gillian described her need to rebuild her reserves ready for this busy time. For her, that meant (a) having more get-up-and-go, (b) enjoying boundless energy and (c) getting those amazing flashes of inspiration and that wonderfully uplifted feeling, every single day. No mean feat!

We talked about everything that was stressing Gillian and draining her energy, from the housework through to her worries about money. What I was keen to find out was how on earth Gillian had managed to pull herself through this stressful period of her life and remain intact at the end of it. When we have long periods under pressure we all find our own little coping strategies, and, while they do their job in the middle of a crisis, in the long-term some of them tend not to be so healthy. I was wondering what Gillian's coping strategy had been.

'Caffeine!' she laughed. 'I probably drink between six and ten Diet Cokes every day!' So that was it. She knew that so much caffeine couldn't be good for her but it was the only way she had been able to get herself through the last year. Some people choose to use coffee as their coping strategy, others nicotine or alcohol; some people work too many hours; others exercise excessively; other people glue themselves to the television or shop till they drop as their way of escaping the real world.

Gillian recognised that it was time for a healthier approach if she was to rise to the challenge of her master's degree and succeed. She didn't just want to drag herself through it in the hope that she'd make it to the other side in one piece – she was fed up of living like that. Gillian wanted to soak up the experience, enjoy the process and excel at the same time. She realised that she would have to change her attitude to lots of things in her life if she was to create the right frame of mind and space in which to excel professionally. Caffeine was the first thing to be tackled and, to top it all, she had only three months to do it.

That night, Gillian made the decision to cut down slowly on her caffeine intake with the intention of cutting it out altogether. Anyone thinking of cutting down their intake of caffeine should consult their doctor first, because, despite the fact that coffee and cola are universally available on our supermarket shelves, it's pretty strong stuff and quitting caffeine suddenly is not generally recommended. Gillian had tried to give up caffeine before and had always gone back to it as she explained in this email.

> Hi, Lynette, I am having a tiny panic. A very strange thing has happened. Last week, I cut out caffeine, which has been an enormous problem in my life for longer than I care to remember. I have got to this stage before with the caffeine and always gone back to drinking it. I am so laid back today I haven't got excited about anything, despite finding three free parking spaces, having a shoe shopping spree and everything going my way rather more than usual. I am so used to scooting around on vodka, diet coke and chocolate that I feel I am losing my personality. I can't possibly live life this calm and I think that's why I always start drinking caffeine again. A miracle has happened over the last few weeks and I don't want to lose the impetus but I literally can't stand this change to being placid, any thoughts?

As Gillian now knows, this is long-term stuff! Any detox programme will tell you that detoxifying your body has its side effects for a while. Gillian wasn't *losing* her personality: she was actually *finding* it. It takes time and energy for the body to rid itself of toxins and the whole process can make you feel pretty lousy; but the end for Gillian was in sight. This was a completely new way of living for her and the 'natural' highs were just around the corner. So determined was she not to sink back into relying on caffeine to feel good that she kept at it. Every session we went through, caffeine became less of a talking point, less of an issue, and we began to tackle other things in her life: her confidence, for instance, her spending habits, the clothes she wore and the state of her wardrobe.

Then, one day, right out of the blue, I received this email:

I wondered if you had advice for some odd symptoms I have been having. I find myself singing or occasionally whistling tunes in the morning, usually from adverts or catchy songs, and smiling in bed at night before I go to sleep. Also, I'm feeling quite energised and 'together' despite being incredibly busy at work and trying to fit in my Master's. Then there's that 'feeling' again which used to be caused by what I now know was a chemical high. A feeling of being excited about the future, happy and all those sorts of things (actually it's a bit like an orgasm – can't describe it but you know when you've had one!).

Gillian had finally reached the point where she was able to feel the natural highs and lows for herself and trust that she was in total control of her life and energy levels. This wasn't just surface feel-good stuff: this was huge life-changing material. It proved that Gillian wasn't only coping on her own but excelling and feeling utterly, orgasmically fantastic in the process!

What's your coping strategy? Is it a healthy one? Is it still working or is it now becoming a hindrance and a pressure stopping you from moving forward in life? Perhaps, as the title of this book suggests, spending money has become your way of coping with pressure. If that's it and you're sinking into the depths of debt, use this tip as your lifeline out. Identify what or whom you lean on and make the decision today to become healthier, to stand on your own two feet and trust your mind and body to provide all the energy and enthusiasm you need.

Make a list of at least five healthier coping strategies that you could choose to adopt from now on. Talking to friends, for instance, walking regularly, reading a good novel and swimming are all excellent ways of bringing together a natural state of balance for your mind and body. Could it be that you need to take regular breaks from your normal routine? Do you have a friend you could stay with in the country or by the sea? Perhaps, it's an escape to the city, to see a show or a comedy play that would really take you out of your stressful life for a few hours. Use your intuition, close your eyes and ask yourself what you need to do. Decide to try something different, really think about how you'd cope more easily, take a big deep breath and organise something today.

Get started right here, right now

This is your incentive to tackle those frighteningly huge jobs, then sit back and breathe in pure satisfaction!

You didn't think when you got up this morning, that this would be the day your life would change, did you? But it's going to happen because the only thing that stands between you and grand success in living are these two things – getting started and never quitting! You can solve your biggest problem by getting started, right here and now.

Robert H. Schuller

Will you do anything to avoid tackling a huge task? Are you a master at procrastinating over jobs you wish would just disappear? Perhaps you'd rather wait until the situation gets really bad before paying someone else to do it for you. If that sounds like you, then you need this strategy.

The 'start anywhere but start somewhere' strategy has been useful not only to me but to my clients as well. Erin wanted to move house but knew that she'd be too embarrassed to bring an estate agent in to value her property in its current state. She was a self-confessed hoarder of all things impractical (and usually broken) and declared that her gift for hoarding and for visiting car boot sales and junk yards had got way out of control, leaving her house in such a mess that she just didn't know where to begin.

Erin did anything rather than spend time in her house, because the state of it bothered her so much. She'd dine in restaurants rather than cook at home and she'd visit yet more junk shops for that high of snapping up a bargain – all to avoid the reality of her situation.

Following our coaching session, Erin realised that not only was she brilliant at avoiding her problem, but she was also spending huge amounts of money in the whole avoidance process! When we added up approximately how much she would spend by dining out and visiting more junk yards in a month, she was amazed, and that session gave Erin the encouragement she needed to tackle her hoarding problem head on.

My first question to her was, 'Where would be the easiest place to start?' Her answer was the downstairs hallway. She decided to hire a skip, bribe a couple of friends to help her and stick on her favourite dance CD. At seven o'clock the following evening she telephoned me, exhausted but elated. They had successfully cleared out three rooms downstairs, hoovered and tidied up, all for the price of a Chinese takeaway! Not only that, but they had had a ball. She'd enjoyed the time spent with her friends, they had done nothing but laugh and joke all day and she felt ready to tackle the rest of the house by nightfall.

Life doesn't need to be complicated, expensive or difficult. The trick is to decide on the least scary place to start and then do just that – start. If that doesn't give you enough incentive, then this just might. First of all, write below what job is nagging at your conscience the most:

_____

Next, write down how you feel about that job:

_____

Next, I'd like you to imagine that you've already done it. The job in hand is actually finished. How are you feeling now?

_____

What would tackling that job today give you?

_____

It's the last question that's likely to be the one that gives you enough of an emotional tug to get you off your backside and into action. Sooner or later, either the pleasure of knowing how you'll feel when it's done or the pain of understanding the effect that procrastination is having on your conscience will spur you into action, but that could take a while. Cut the whole dilly-dallying process in half and answer the questions above.

Which job have you been putting off? Which task seems totally insurmountable at the moment? What is it that you're avoiding and which clever little avoidance tactics have you been using to get out of dealing with that job? Be brave today. Start tackling a project. Start *anywhere* and make a dent in it, be it the housework, the laundry, the filing, the thank-you letters, those tax forms that urgently need completing, the essay you've been meaning to get done – just get on and do it. Do something today. Start *somewhere* – and you'll be surprised at the difference it makes.

Bloke psychology

Not getting on with your man? Arguing over mundane tasks? Don't give up. Read this first and speak his language.

Have you ever wondered whether you and your man speak completely different languages? Well here's the news: you do. We act so differently, and sometimes it's difficult to see the logic on both sides, but you ask any woman and she'll tell you that she just cannot walk past a piece of thread on the carpet without stopping and picking it up, while a man wouldn't notice it was there if it was waving a red flag at him! They think differently from us, see things (or don't see things!) differently, and their versions of words and ours are sometimes worlds apart.

To help with this massive difference in logic, I have developed the Three-Step Bloke Rule. It's something that all women should be aware of and it will prove to be a life-saver on a day-to-day basis. Here it is:

1. know that not all blokes have peripheral vision;
2. know that not all blokes respond to subtle dropping of hints; and

3. know that most blokes don't respond to criticism or putdowns.

First, peripheral vision. I was recently told by someone (yes, a man!), that men's vision is basically tunnelled. Now that's not generally a problem, except when they're looking for something. We've all been busy doing something in the house when he's shouted, 'Where's my [whatever]?' We'll have shouted back either exactly where it is or at least its approximate whereabouts and expect him to look for it. Our mistake is in not assuming the tunnel-vision thing. Once you do, you'll no longer cry out with frustration at how 'manlike' he is for not being able to find it.

When we say, 'It's in the drawer', he's going to open the drawer and expect to see it immediately. Now what we need to start saying is, 'Look around inside the drawer.' Then you are telling him specifically that he needs to rummage about in the drawer to find whatever is lost. It helps to be specific, or as specific as we can – and, let's face it, we can be pretty specific when we choose to be! Women's vision, it seems, is much more peripheral, so, when we look for things, we see them out of the corner of our eyes. Men, I'm told, don't immediately see the stuff that's in their peripheral vision. Apparently, it's really not their fault at all. They're not trying to be difficult; nor are they just plain stupid. It's actually part of their make-up and, rather than moan at them, maybe it's time for us to be more precise about the whole 'finding things' process.

Now on to 'subtle hint dropping'. The fairer sex are masters at this, having studied the fine art for hundreds of years. However good we become at it, though, it may not always be picked up by your bloke – and that's when the trouble starts. This tip is about assuming that the technique of dropping subtle hints won't work. Girls, it's just easier and saves hours, even days, of frustration when they're just not getting the hint. Instead, be straight. Don't beat about the bush. Ask the question – and ask it using the right language. There are two phrases to remember, 'Will you' and 'You are'.

A client of mine, Elaine, is a mother with a three-month-old baby and she has a loving partner. However, much as Elaine would have loved the offer of help with their son, offers from Dad weren't exactly forthcoming. One day, she voiced her concerns and told her partner that, unless he started to take more of an active role in looking after their baby, she was concerned that they wouldn't develop a bond. His answer? 'Well, you do everything, so what's the point in offering?'

It seems that, when she constantly hints that she'd like help or when she gets sarcastic at the lack of attention, her partner perceives it as nagging. However, asking a straight question such as, 'Will you please change the baby?' or, 'Would you kindly take out the rubbish?' is seen merely as a request for help and he willingly moves into action. The other thing to remember in the whole direct-question approach is to use 'would you/will you' instead of 'could you/can you'.

The latter actually comes across as 'are you capable of…?', which of course questions his masculinity and capability – and, trust me, no man wants either of those qualities to be questioned. The 'would you/will you' approach, however, simply asks whether they would be prepared to do the task in hand and, of course, most of the time (unless the footie, the golf or the rugby is on!), it has a much more positive effect. We girls may find it hard to hear the difference – but try saying 'Could you marry me?' instead of 'Will you marry me?' and you'll definitely hear the difference!

The 'you are' phrase is just as important, and once women know this secret, conversations will be transformed. Men need to know that we think they're decent, loving, kind individuals and we can let them know this by altering our language. Gabrielle Blackman-Shepphard is an executive coach who specialises in coaching men. She says, 'Instead of saying "Thank you – that was a nice thing to do" we could use the more powerful "Thank you – you are such a thoughtful man".' This brings the compliment back to them as people. It praises them and not just the action.

Now we girls do this a lot, without even realising it. We use 'you are' in the negative sense a lot, and it's this that has to stop. We'll say, 'You're so thoughtless' or 'You're just arrogant' without a second thought; and, ladies, it needs one – a second thought, that is! It's time to refine our language and listen to the words we say. We instinctively know how to hurt but we have trouble when we try to build up our men. When you next want to compliment your other half (and make sure you do – every day), start with 'You are', then follow with the praise, and you'll see him grow taller with pride!

Then there is the criticism or putdown method, which we seem to have cultivated over the years along with the subtle-dropping-of-hints method. Granted, it's usually through frustration, but it's not a healthy habit. It wouldn't work on us, so why should we expect it to work on them?

Men have fragile egos and despite their tough, testos-teroned exterior, they're just as sensitive as we are and they respond no better to criticism or putdowns than we would. No amount of 'You're just lazy', 'You're afraid of hard work' or 'You're downright inconsiderate' is going to spur your bloke into a frenzy of action ready to pull his weight – or, if it does, it will be a poor half-hearted effort giving rise to a swift, 'I might as well have done it myself' from you. Why should they help or aim to do a good job when we've put them down before they've even started?

Whether it's a male boss who annoys you, a male colleague you're not getting on with or a partner at home who accuses you of nagging all the time, follow the Three-Step Bloke Rule and finish with praise and compliments – and you'll be amazed at what can be achieved.

I want that job

Want to change jobs but hate the interview bit? Would you love to earn more money but can't stand the embarrassment of losing the power of speech at the interview? Use this strategy to switch interview stress around in minutes.

For most of us, our job defines who we are. When we introduce ourselves, after giving our name, we tend to identify ourselves by our job. When most people are making polite chitchat at social events, their opening line is, 'What do you do?' Our job is a hugely important part of who we are, how we are perceived by others and how we perceive ourselves. What does your job say about you? Are you proud to tell people what you do – or do you cringe every time someone asks?

Our jobs and careers are what pay the bills, give us our lifestyles, our standard of living, the clothes we wear, and they also dictate where we can afford to go on holiday. It's no wonder they can be so stressful. Our jobs and the money we earn tell people an awful lot about who we are and how educated and confident we are, so it's absolutely vital to be in a job that you not only enjoy but that gives you a lifestyle and image you're happy with. If your job doesn't match the lifestyle and image you desire, you could find yourself spending on that credit card to *buy* the standard of living and image that you really want to portray.

We're under constant pressure to be successful. Advertising creates a deep desire within us to appear to have 'made it'. We prove how successful we are by the houses we live in, the cars we drive and the clothes we wear, so there's no wonder we find the green-eyed monster within us eyeing up our best friend's 'his 'n' hers' basins when we visit the loo or making mental notes of the shades of cream she's so cleverly chosen for her hallway.

Image means a lot, whether we like it or not. We know we shouldn't be envious of what other people earn or how much their bathrooms cost to refit; we know deep down that we should coo and make other admiring noises in the right places and just be thankful for our health – but it's hard! We constantly want more, and, with so much choice, no sooner have we redecorated in rich creams and browns, as per our favourite magazine, than it seems that slate grey is back in and it all has to be redone. The bottom line is that if you love 'a certain lifestyle', and your job doesn't provide the income to sustain your desire for leather sofas, twice-yearly holidays in Bali and designer cashmere, you could be heading for trouble.

Some time ago, Jacky was deeply unhappy in her job. She worked long hours in what she called a soulless environment and was getting paid far less than her friends. They all had jobs they loved, jobs that gave them salaries to match, and Jacky admitted to getting more than ten thousand pounds in debt trying to keep up with them. She'd go out shopping with them, pay for lunch sometimes and buy the designer clothes and accessories that her friends could afford. They were totally unaware of the debt she was running up and she realised that she had to take some action soon to get the situation under control.

Jacky told me she admired her friends' confidence and ability to get the jobs they wanted. They'd see a new job advertised, get themselves together and just go for the interview. Nine times out of ten, they would end up with salary increases and demanding and interesting new jobs – but, each time they did, her confidence in her ability to do the same fell a little further. When I asked what her worst nightmare was when it came to changing jobs, she said, without hesitation, that it was the interview stage.

Jacky had always hated interviews: she fumbled for words; her usual sense of humour and easy charm vanished; she'd come out in a cold sweat (dreading that telltale clammy interview handshake); and she turned into a gibbering wreck by the time the interview day came. She'd even been known to cry off appointments through fear. Consequently, she never saw herself changing jobs and was just grateful to have one in the first place! This had to change and it was this strategy that changed Jacky almost instantly.

I asked her how she'd go about interviewing a company that she may want to work for. Jacky said she had no idea and wouldn't even know where to start. So that first session we came up with a series of questions that she might ask if the interview were the reversal of the usual – if she were interviewing the company instead of being interviewed by them. This is the list we came up with:

- Who would I be working for?

- Who would I be sharing an office with?

- Do you allow flexitime?

- What opportunities are there for promotion?

- What qualities do you value most in your employees?

- How much is the starting salary?

- Are there opportunities to work from home?

- What are the benefits of working for your company?

These were Jacky's questions, and yours may be different; but the important part is that Jacky had never even considered the idea of interviewing a company and had never entertained the thought that, even if she was offered a job, she might not want to work there. When you go to an interview, your bosses are as much on show as you are. If you consider yourself to be one of *the* most valuable employees around, that will come across, leaving your potential bosses trying to impress *you*.

When you next go for an interview, think about asking yourself these questions:

- Did they look like friendly people?

- Did they have a sense of humour?

- Did you get shown around the office where you'd be based?

- Did they smile during the interview?

- Did they put you at your ease?

- What was the feel of the office?

- What was your intuition telling you?

Women particularly have a very keen sense of intuition. I've spoken about this many times before and it's important to listen to your inner voice at this stage. If you feel a sense of excitement, then it may well be the right job for you. But, if you can't wait to get out of there, your intuition is probably right, so let your legs do the talking and don't look back.

I have never seen anyone so enthusiastic as Jacky was to get her hands on the appointments page! She bought a paper on the way home from our session and applied for two new jobs that afternoon. They both had higher salaries than she was used to and she was excited for the first time in years. She wanted to find out how other companies worked. She was now curious as to whether she'd get a nicer, more amiable boss and whether she'd get better perks. She called me two weeks later after her second interview. She'd been offered the job on the spot and, to cap it all, it was the higher-paid job of the two. Jacky's posture improved, she told me, and her body language and eye contact couldn't have been more positive. The interviewer was charming and any pre-interview nerves disappeared as quickly as her ability to speak eloquently arrived.

Jacky was convinced that her attitude change had been the key to her success, enabling her to land a job that she loves. Her salary has increased, her debt is coming down and she recently told me that she doesn't even feel the need to spend the huge amounts she did before to keep up with her friends.

Her job title and work environment have given her a huge boost and genuinely elevated her status and ego. She's proud of what she does now and also what she earns.

Remember that the first rule of interviews is that *you* are interviewing *them*; they're the ones on the stage, not you. Just remember, you might not even want to work there.

The dating game

Do you flirt outrageously and then run for the hills when you're asked out on a date? Would you rather de-flea your next-door neighbour's cat than go out on a date? Well these tips may just rev up your love life!

Dating can be a minefield. You don't know their past and first dates feel like nothing more than question-and-answer sessions. They can bore you senseless with office drivel as they attempt to sound articulate and entertaining while you've got one eye very firmly on the clock, ready to run for the ladies' to send your best friend the 'emergency SOS' text!

It's no wonder some people just avoid dating like the plague, preferring to flirt their way through life without ever having to go through those uncomfortable 'will he/won't he' scenarios. Many women would much rather sit at home with the dog and the remote control than overanalyse what his latest text *really* meant. Well, if that's you and you're happy as you are, great; but if you'd secretly really love to be a 'they' rather than a 'she', if meals for one seem more and more unappetising and you're desperate for an excuse to throw caution to the wind and replace those Bridget Jones undies with sexy little thongs, then think about this!

Christa is a fortysomething who decided to bite the bullet and go all out to meet new people, determined to gather the confidence to go out on dates again. She was fed up with the fact that her teenage daughter had a better social life than she did. She hadn't been out on a date in over seven years, preferring to put all her energy into raising her daughter. But, now that her daughter was nearly grown up, Christa was ready to start thinking of herself again. She was excited but very nervous about the whole dating scene, cringing at the thought of speed dating and singles parties. She felt totally unprepared to enter this new phase and we worked together on areas that would need to change, in order for her to feel ready to enjoy the prospect of a date.

The first thing we spoke about was the fact that Christa was famous for turning down outings with friends. At heart, she is quite shy and going to parties and gatherings fills her with horror rather than excitement. That was the first challenge and Christa decided that, from now on, she would accept every invitation she could, even those where she wasn't necessarily going to meet a man. Over the coming weeks, she started to go to the cinema again, went out to dinner with various friends and generally started to 'be seen' again. Just before our second session, Christa revamped her wardrobe, by decluttering it and buying a few new trendy items. Finally, she felt ready to say yes to her friend's fortieth-birthday party. She would know no one there except the birthday girl herself, so Christa and I talked over three techniques for enjoying a party instead of dreading it:

- learning simple flirting techniques;
- learning how to make easy small talk; and
- learning how to extricate yourself from the inevitable party bore.

Christa and I spoke about all kinds of flirting techniques she could use, such as making direct eye contact and holding it for a little longer than usual, touching someone's arm when speaking to them, smiling, paying a man a compliment and asking questions about his 'other half', just to check whether there is one! If your chosen one hasn't got the hint by then, move on!

As for small talk, Christa's nightmare scenario was that the conversation would dry up, leaving her with an embarrassing silence. This need never happen, as everyone's favourite subject is themselves! Ask about their lives and it's an open invitation to chat about something interesting – them!

This brings us on to the next and quite vital strategy: how to extricate ourselves when Mr Boring starts detailing his curriculum vitae and he's still only up to 1985! There are all kinds of excuses that you can use, from glancing at the clock, saying you have to be somewhere, to saying, 'Oh, there's someone I need to have a word with; thanks for chatting to me – have a nice evening.' You can use whichever exit strategy suits you but the general rule of etiquette is that there's no need to be rude and you don't need to put someone down as you finish your conversation. Smile and tell them you've enjoyed talking to them before moving on. There's no doubt this takes a bit of practise, but practise is exactly what Christa decided to do, so she rehearsed exit strategies with her daughter. She even picked up a few tips, too!

Christa went off to her party with all her strategies, making eye contact, asking people about themselves and excusing herself from conversations when needed – she was a great hit.

If you're fed up with cocoa for one at bedtime, go on, take control, make the decision to start going out more, get into the habit of talking to people you don't know very well and practise those old flirting techniques. You'll be surprised at just how much fun dating can be.

Complain and get heard

Are you the type of person who just wants to hide under the table when one of your party complains? Have you lost hundreds of pounds over the years just because you lacked the confidence and know-how to stand up and be heard? Then listen up with these tips and never feel cheated again.

No one wants to complain about services or products. What we'd really love is for there to be no real need to complain. This strategy isn't about turning you from meek fieldmouse into professional complainer from hell in one easy step, but there's a fair balance to be had and this is how to get it.

Complaining takes courage and confidence and, if you're not the kind of person who enjoys making a fuss in a busy shop or restaurant, my guess is that you've quietly slipped out of both on more than a few occasions rather than say anything. I remember as a teenager shopping with my mother for shoes for my little brother. The shop assistant could find only one shoe of the pair that my brother wanted, so she offered it to my mum for half-price. As my mum gasped in amazement and asked for the manager, I scuttled out of the shop, crimson with adolescent embarrassment, and hid until it was all over, vowing never to go shopping with her again!

Complaining for the sake of it is not recommended, but standing up for the right to good service and courteous shop assistants is a must – and there's no reason why you shouldn't expect both.

During one of my coaching sessions with Lorna, she winced as she told me how she'd bought a pair of expensive trousers, only to wear them once and have them shrink at least two sizes in the wash. Wearing them again was an impossibility unless she went on a starvation diet and she didn't know anyone small enough to pass them on to. So there they were, a perfectly good, almost brand-new, beautiful pair of trousers, worn once, never to go near her thighs again!

Lorna felt unable to go back to the shop as she assumed that they'd probably say she hadn't followed the washing instructions. She couldn't prove that she had but, in fact, she had taken particular care to check what cycle to use. Lorna wasn't only cross with the shop for selling her a substandard pair of trousers but she was more cross with herself for not having the guts to make a complaint.

She told me she'd never been very good at complaining, but I suggested that this might be a good time to think about learning. After all, she had a valid reason for wanting a refund, so she decided to phone the shop. We talked through her strategy, which was to ask to speak to the manager, to stay very calm, go through the facts and tell him or her just what she expected. Most managers want to get complaints sorted out quickly and satisfactorily because they want you to come back. If you've ever been on a management course, you'll know that, from a manager's point of view, handled correctly and responsibly, a complaint can be a brilliant opportunity to turn an angry customer into one of your biggest fans.

Lorna needed to be in the right frame of mind to make that call so she wrote down exactly what she wanted to say and what she wanted them to do about her complaint. She made herself comfortable in her lounge and made sure that her family were out of earshot before making the call. The manager was very respectful and admitted that several pairs of those particular trousers had been brought back with the same fault. Not only did he agree to refund the cost to her card but also said he would send her a voucher for ten pounds for the disappointment.

Follow these top tips when you need to complain and get the results you want:

- If in a restaurant, complain at the time – the manager can't do anything about your lukewarm meal after you've eaten it!

- If a product has gone wrong, take it back to the shop as soon as you can, with the receipt.

- Always ask to speak to the manager or someone in charge – sales assistants generally have very little authority and may not be able to deal with your complaint.

- Be polite, don't raise your voice and certainly don't swear – you wouldn't respond to verbal abuse, and neither will shop assistants and managers.

- Be firm but courteous about what you'd like them to do and, when you've voiced your request, stop speaking, even if there's a silence – let the manager speak first and allow him or her to consider your request.

- If you don't get the answer you're looking for quickly, persist and be prepared to come to an agreement.

Complaining needn't be a major drama. In fact, you might be surprised at how well you're treated. Stop berating yourself for money you've wasted by not complaining. From now on, take the bull by the horns and be brave.

Flashes of inspiration

Do you find it hard to cope with stressful situations? Do you wish you had an instant remedy to calm you down? Well, if you find yourself losing your temper when your patience is tested to the very limit, you'll love this little gem.

Imagine how different your life might be if you could say just one word to yourself to make all that stress and tension wash right over you, leaving you feeling as refreshed as that woman in the Timotei advert! Well, if you think it's impossible, you haven't met Angela.

If you were to drop in on Angela, her six-month-old daughter and two-year-old son on a busy weekday, you might find her with her head deep in a kitchen cupboard. Searching for chocolate? Wondering where the headache tablets are, maybe? No, she'll be reading flash cards! Angela has all kinds of messages that she's written to herself and put on flash cards taped to the inside of the kitchen cupboard. She knows she looks quite mad, head stuck in a cupboard chanting to herself and practising deep-breathing exercises, but it's those flash cards and messages that are keeping her sane, with two demanding toddlers and a house to run. This is what they say:

- 'Don't shout'
- 'Count to twenty'
- 'Get down to his level'
- 'No negotiation'
- 'Say his name before telling him off'
- 'Keep eye contact'
- 'Remember, he's a little person'
- 'This won't last for ever!'

In the middle of a temper tantrum when enough is enough, instead of losing her cool, Angela takes a few minutes to read her flash cards and calm herself down, and then she deals with the situation. It works for her, reminding her how best to deal with stress – and it could help you, too.

You don't have to have children running around to appreciate the value of these little cards, though. Long before children, or even her husband, came along, Angela used flash cards. She'd have happy and positive messages stuck to the walls of her flat, to encourage and calm her when she'd had a bad day. They are a brilliant way to focus your energy and thoughts in a constructive, positive manner that means you'll get through the day looking slightly less frazzled and frayed around the edges.

Cora took inspiration from this when her twin daughters were going through their teens. Frequent scenes of door slamming and shouting were a normal everyday occurrence and utter pandemonium reigned until she decided to put flash cards into practice. On one of the quieter days sitting with her daughters over dinner, she suggested the 'Flash Card Code'. She bought pens and paper and, after dinner, all three girls sat and wrote out flash cards that they thought would help each of them to calm down and plant their feet very firmly on the ground along with their tempers.

They wrote things such as 'Remember to love', 'I respect my mum', 'Calm' and 'Breathe'. The girls even decided to put a flash card on their bedroom door, announcing their mood first thing in the morning so everyone knew when to 'handle with care'!

This not only helped the girls individually but it also helped them both to be more considerate towards their mother. They even turned their music down one day when she put a flash card on her bedroom door stating quite clearly that she wasn't having a great day.

If you had a few flash cards of your own for you and your family, or even your work colleagues, what would they say? Where would you keep them? In what circumstances do you think they might help?

Write five short flash-card messages below that you can refer to when times are tough. Look at them often, breathe deeply when you read them and, for those few minutes, try to block everything and everyone else out. Concentrate on the one or two words you're reading. Next time your patience is wearing thin, you'll calm down in a flash!

_____

_____

_____

_____

_____

Make magnificent mistakes

Do you wander around life always feeling as if you're making one massive mistake after another? Would you love to stop that dreaded cycle? Here's how.

We've all made mistakes. After all, we're only human. Some days are better than others and some decisions are better than others – it's perfectly normal. However, there are a few people in this world, and you may think you're one of them, who constantly make mistakes, time after time, whether it's the wrong job, the wrong partner, the wrong house or the wrong financial venture. If you have a million stories of how you could have done it better, trusted a different person or saved yourself a fortune by choosing a different financial opportunity, then this chapter has been written just for you.

If making mistakes has become part of your identity and people constantly urge you to think before you act, then take heed: make one fewer mistake today and stop the treadmill.

How do you make magnificent mistakes? Magnificent mistakes are different from your normal everyday mistake. Magnificent mistakes are those that you learn from. Maybe you're the type of person who makes the same mistake over and over again. It's easy to think that next time things will be different, but I'm sure you've heard the saying, 'If you always do the same thing, you'll continue to get the same results' – and it's absolutely true.

The only way that you stop the cycle of making mistakes is to learn from them and listen hard for warning bells next time.

The questions below could be the key to breaking that cycle, if you answer them as truthfully as your conscience will allow. These questions should be answered in the privacy of your own space to be most effective. None of us like to admit we've been naïve or stupid and we certainly don't want to hear it from other people, so this is the reason you need to be sure no one will see your answers. That way you can be absolutely honest with yourself.

Another huge part of this confessional is that you have to be prepared to put that precious ego of yours to one side for a few minutes. Egos stop us from admitting our faults and help us to come up with excuses. It's no good if you're going to answer these questions with sentences that start with 'But if …' and 'It wasn't my fault …'

While it's true that we don't always consciously notice fraudulent people or situations, our subconscious mind will usually tip us off in very subtle ways, if it thinks that something is amiss. It is the conscious mind that then chooses whether to accept that information and pick up on the subtle hint. That's why it is this subconscious voice that needs to be heeded and it's your intuition that you need to take much more notice of next time. In order to be more aware of that deeper level, you first need to take off your egotistical hat, put it to one side and admit that you probably heard warning bells long before you chose to listen to them and put a stop to the event.

I've spoken to numerous divorcees, for instance, who have all told me, 'I knew I shouldn't have married him.' One woman even said, 'As I said my vows, I knew I was making the biggest mistake of my life.' Why go through with decisions you feel are wrong? Why put yourself in situations where you know you're making yet another mammoth mistake? Perhaps it's because you haven't had the chance to sit down and note exactly what went wrong last time. Once you do that you are able to build into your subconscious a specific set of alarms that your conscious mind is able to recognise. Once you have those alarms in place, as with a well-secured building, you'll know exactly when one goes off, in what area it's been triggered and how to go about dealing with that threat.

These are the questions that will help you to set up your own personal security system. Remember to take your ego in your hands and carefully place it by your side. Don't worry, you can have it back when you've finished!

Remember the last time you made a huge mistake? Try to remember the things that were going on in your life at the time and the people who were around you, and then answer the following questions:

What was the first decision you made in the beginning, that led to the mistake?

_____

_____

When exactly do you remember making that specific decision?

_____

_____

Did anyone ask you to make it?

_____

_____

Did you feel pressured into giving an answer at that very moment?

_____

_____

If yes, what tactics did that person use to make sure that you gave an answer there and then?

_____

_____

What was your intuition telling you?

_____

_____

When did you start to feel as if you may have made a mistake?

_____

_____

Now you know that you did make a mistake, what could you have said or done differently?

_____

_____

What other information did you really need to feel able to make that decision with more certainty and clarity?

_____

_____

What have you learned from that mistake?

_____

_____

Which warning signs are you now aware of that would stop you from making a similar mistake in the future?

_____

_____

List five alarm bells that you need to be aware of next time:

1. _____

2. _____

3. _____

4. _____

5. _____

What you should have now are five ways in which you could learn from your past mistakes and avoid making them in the future. Oh, and by the way, if you haven't already, you can put your ego back on now if you like! To learn from mistakes, you need to be able to stand up and admit that you made one in the first place. Don't let other people take responsibility for your clangers. Own them, be aware of them and then take the responsibility for them. We teach children all the time to own up to their mistakes – now it's your turn.

When you've admitted those mistakes and taken responsibility for them, it's up to you to learn from them and build your own alarm system to stop you from making them again.

You don't have to be the type of person who makes mistakes all the time. You could change completely – it is entirely possible. You could become someone who trusts their decisions and learns from past mistakes.

Lastly, you can finally put that big wet fish down and stop slapping yourself around the head with it. Don't beat yourself up any more. Instead, decide to admit, own and learn.

Promised promises

Do you find yourself making promises that you know you probably won't keep? If you can't understand why you do it, let alone know how to stop, this is the strategy that will make broken promises a thing of the past.

Promises are made and carried out the world over with no problem at all – but there are some of us who are infamous for doing exactly the opposite.

If you're a consistent promise maker and breaker, you'll recognise that horrible pang in the pit of your stomach every time you think about it – and it's that feeling that this strategy will banish. This tip will help you to understand why you make false promises in the first place and it will also help you fulfil future promises every time.

First, people who make promises they know they're not going to keep do so for many reasons but, in my view, they all come down to just two:

- they feel backed into a corner and under pressure to give an answer immediately; and
- they want people to like them.

When people feel backed into a corner, they often lack the confidence to make the other person wait while they consider their request. So what happens? So keen are they to get the other person off their back and be left alone, that they will promise to move heaven and earth for a quiet life. Whether they can actually deliver or not is an entirely different matter and they'll usually spend days worrying about how they're going to carry out the task.

People also make promises because they want to be liked and included. We humans, by our very nature, love to be liked and accepted in society and sometimes a promise is all it takes to enter that world of acceptance. If you recognise that you behave in this way, you need to work out a way of entering that cosy world of acceptance in other ways. When promises are broken, people soon learn that you're not to be trusted and you're straight out of the circle of acceptance anyway, so the whole exercise has been a waste of time and energy.

There is just one strategy that covers every eventuality. Just a few words at the beginning of any promise protects you from breaking your word. By starting a sentence with 'I can't promise anything, but I'd love to …' or 'If at all possible, I will …' puts a condition on the promise. It's like putting a protective boundary around the promise and the person you're making it to. Starting sentences with, 'I try never to make a promise I can't keep', for instance, means you're upfront and honest, and very few people can argue against that. Being totally honest in the first place shows maturity, integrity and reliability, and you avoid being labelled as someone who can't be trusted.

Yasmin frequently got into trouble when she made promises to her clients, friends, colleagues and family. She hates saying no and would rather promise to walk on hot coals than disappoint. So eager is she to please that she's been known to avoid people for months because she knows she cannot fulfil the promises she's made.

Yasmin agreed to try two new strategies. The first was to put a condition on the promise next time she felt herself about to make one, and she agreed to say, 'I'm going to try, but I can't promise.' The second, was to learn to trust herself again. Yasmin was so used to being regarded by her friends as a promise breaker that she would often talk herself into breaking promises before she'd even made them. I asked Yasmin to practise a little positive self-talk and got her to repeat 'I keep all my promises' as many times as she could. This etches onto your subconscious the fact that you're turning over a new leaf and makes promises easier to keep. Very soon, you'll start to trust your own word and then everyone else can follow.

I spoke to Yasmin two weeks after she had put her new plan into action and she proudly told me she'd kept every promise she made. The key is honesty. It's not always possible to move mountains but, if you swear that you can, others may believe you. It's best to be straightforward and try not to give your word unless you're sure you can deliver.

Susan, on the other hand, is a genuine promise maker. At the time of making a promise, she'll mean it with every fibre of her being, but, before she's even finished the conversation, she's forgotten what she promised to do. Susan is a busy working mum and often has to multitask just to get through the day. While talking to friends, she could be chopping vegetables for dinner, supervising her children and letting the dog out all at the same time! When Susan forgets promises, she's mortified that she's let her friends down *again*, so I asked her a question: 'If you always kept your promises what would you do differently?' She said that she'd have a book of promises and write them all down. A fantastic idea! Susan bought a small note-book to fit in her handbag and from now on whenever she makes a promise she writes it down, checking them daily. She is thrilled with her new strategy, as are her friends and family.

Another group of promise breakers are those who don't even realise they've made a promise in the first place. A simple 'Yes, we'll do that', for instance, may sound very much like a promise to your friend, when in fact it may just be an enthusiastic answer on your part. The tip here is to be more aware of what you say. People misunderstand all the time, so be careful, try to be as literal as you can and clarify things if need be.

Finally, while it's not recommended to go around breaking promises willy-nilly, there are times when you may need to. We women do try to please the entire population and their grannies and sometimes we make promises that end up plaguing us when it all gets too much. There is, however, a code of conduct for breaking promises and, once you know what it is, it will seem so much easier.

It's called the 'Apologise and Explain Code'. When life takes over good intentions and we find ourselves drowning in a sea of unkept promises, it's time to apologise and explain. Again, honesty is important and it's certainly valued when you're letting people down. If you follow the 'Apologise and Explain Code', most people won't object. Make the phone call or write a short note, but, whichever way you choose to communicate, tell your friend you're genuinely sorry you won't be able to keep your promise and explain why.

The worst thing you can do is never to mention your promise again in the hope that your friend will forget about it. They won't! It will sit and fester in both of your minds, creating bad feeling and ruining an otherwise perfectly good friendship.

Be a reliable promise maker instead of a consistent promise breaker with these rules:

- be honest;

- put conditions on your promises;

- write down your promises so you don't forget them; and

- break promises only by using the 'Apologise and Explain Code' for minimum fallout.

Stairway to happiness

Do you go through periods of feeling very down and depressed? Do you find it hard to pull yourself through stressful times without seriously affecting your mood? This could be a new approach.

Depression has been described by many people as a feeling of being in another room while the world is continuing without you. It's a very lonely feeling of being totally isolated, even if you're surrounded by loving friends and family. There are a variety of reasons why people feel depressed and even those who seem upbeat can feel awful at times too.

If you think you could be depressed, it's important to face it and deal with it. You can do that by visiting your GP. Counselling may help too, as may speaking in confidence to a friend. Of course, complementary-health practitioners can be great in stressful times. It's important to recognise at this point that there are varying degrees of depression, from 'normal depression', if you like, when you may have periods of feeling swamped by life and be generally unable to cope, to 'clinical depression', which may need medical intervention. This strategy is aimed at people who generally cope with all life throws at them reasonably well. This is the type of strategy that helps you build in a safeguard to stop 'normal depression' deteriorating into a more serious state.

If you look closely, there will be a pattern that takes you from feeling perfectly OK and in control to feeling completely depressed, crying all the time and unable to work and function as usual. The end result doesn't just happen overnight. There are a whole load of telltale signs in the middle and this strategy will help you and those around you to identify those signs. When you have recognised your personal signs, you'll be much more aware that you're starting to act differently and you'll be able to do something about it before you hit rock bottom.

Imagine a flight of stairs. Picture them clearly in your mind. How many stairs does your staircase have? There may be twenty, for instance, or there may be just four – it's totally up to you. Just close your eyes, concentrate and visualise the staircase. The top of the staircase is where you're feeling fantastic. This is where you want to stay. You're happy, you're smiling and you're coping with everyday stresses well. The bottom stair, on the other hand, is where you are when life's got on top of you and you feel unable to cope. The stairs in between signify all the telltale symptoms of how you feel as you sink into a state. For instance, the symptom for the first stair down from the top might be that you cry easily. The one for the next stair down from that might be that you blow small inconsequential things out of proportion. And the next stair down may signify that you spend too much or drink too much. The symptoms are yours, so please don't feel obliged to use the ones I've suggested. Yours will be unique to you and shouldn't be compared to anyone else's.

When you analyse and recognise the stages of depression, you are much more likely to be able to stop and find help next time you feel yourself making your way down that staircase. In fact, even with these symptoms in place, you may have to rely on your family and friends to tell you when they notice that you're going down. It's not always easy to tell, especially when you're the one having the symptoms.

Soo has found this stairway very helpful. At her first coaching session, she described to me how she found it so easy to go from Olympic medal status in happiness right down to Olympic medal status in depression and self-pity. She didn't realise she was there until it was too late. By the time she realised, it would be an enormous struggle for her to bring herself back up the staircase and every step made her feel as if she were climbing a mountain. She told me that this process seemed to happen very quickly but, when we worked out the individual stages, she realised it took longer than she thought. These were Soo's stairs:

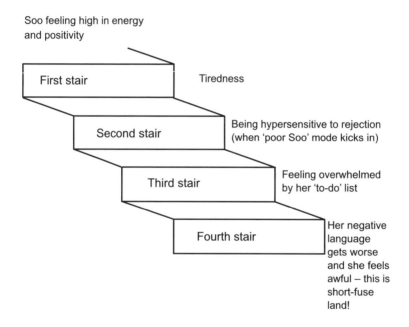

Soo feeling high in energy and positivity

First stair

Tiredness

Second stair

Being hypersensitive to rejection (when 'poor Soo' mode kicks in)

Third stair

Feeling overwhelmed by her 'to-do' list

Fourth stair

Her negative language gets worse and she feels awful – this is short-fuse land!

For Soo, this has been a very important learning curve, as she now easily recognises the symptoms on stairs one to four. What I then asked Soo to do was to sit down with her two teenage daughters and explain that she needed their help. I asked her to explain the stair-way system and the symptoms at each level. Her daughters' job was to notice her symptoms and then make Soo aware of them. Soo asked them to help her identify her first symptom, i.e. when she looked tired, lacked energy and of course (probably the easiest one) got irritable!

This was a different approach for her, and I reminded her of the importance of listening to them when they flagged up her symptoms. This system wasn't going to work if she brushed off their help by saying, 'Oh I'm fine, stop fussing!' Previously, Soo had carried on to the point of exhaustion, refusing to believe she wasn't coping and struggling on regardless. She needed to put herself first and be aware of her symptoms in order to continue to be the capable woman she truly is. This method prevents her from sinking to the point of no return, but only if she takes notice of her girls. This method now gives her the time to put her backup plans into place well before she is unable to function properly.

Next, Soo needed a plan of action for when her first symptom appeared – and this was her personal three-step action plan.

Step 1: To acknowledge and recognise that her daughters were right and that she was tired. She agreed to be kind to herself and say, 'I am tired, I am my best friend, what do I need to do now to nourish and nurture myself?'

This was a fantastic question for Soo to ask her body, and again she needed to be prepared to listen to the answer. This is where Soo's intuition came in. The first answer that came into her mind was probably the one she needed to listen to.

Step 2: To do whatever her body most craved and, if that was to lie down for an hour, that's what she decided to do.

Step 3: To make sure that she was properly hydrated. As I've mentioned before, tiredness can be a sign of dehydration, so it is vital to make sure that your body is properly hydrated to keep it functioning well.

With these three actions, Soo is now able to bring herself back to the top of the stairway quickly and easily.

As always, this is where you get to do some thinking! I'd like you to fill in the stairway below with the symptoms that you feel best indicate when you're getting more and more stressed. There are only four stairs here but feel free to add more if you need to.

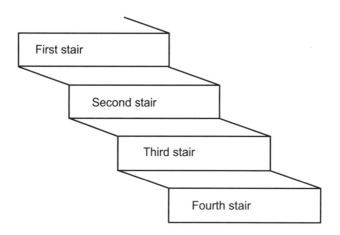

First stair

Second stair

Third stair

Fourth stair

The next part of this process is to come up with three backup plans, as Soo did. Think about the kinds of things that would bring you back up to the top of the stairs. When you're ready, write them here:

1. _____

2. _____

3. _____

Teach yourself to recognise when life gets tough. Depression is more common than you think. It's nothing to be ashamed of and it can happen to anyone at any stage of life. Understand how you need to respond to it and it won't be the frighteningly huge mountain it used to be.

Friends reconnected

How well do you actually know those people you consider to be your close friends? How often do you really get to talk to those closest to you and find out what makes them tick, what they love and what connection you both have? Feel the connection with this tip.

I was sent an email recently. You've probably seen them. The idea is that you answer the questions on the email about yourself – what you like, what you hate, that sort of thing – and then you mail it back to the person who sent it to you. The idea behind this is that they learn something about you and you learn something about them. As yours probably does, my computer gets swamped with circular emails, jokes and spam, most of which I delete very quickly. However, I kept this one. I actually thought it was a really good way of connecting with my friends.

Now this won't be everyone's cup of tea, and, if it's not yours, feel free to skip this chapter completely and move on. If you're intrigued, though, and want an interesting and fun way to bond with your friends, you'll want to read this.

You'll probably have filled in questionnaires like this as a teenager. After all, back then, you probably had more time to yourself than you knew what to do with. Adults don't have as much time, which is why friendships fade and whole years go by before we've even noticed. This exercise will take a few minutes, but could well be the excuse you need to contact an old friend and say hello.

I've compiled a questionnaire, based on the one I received, for you to copy to your friends and family. Unfortunately, I can't say where or from whom this idea originated, as I really don't know, but I *can* say a big thank-you to the person who started this. Take two minutes to answer the questions below, copy it for a friend, ask for their answers and reconnect with those you love.

1. What's on your desk?

   _____

2. What's most important to you in life?

   _____

3. What's your biggest dream?

   _____

4. What's the worst feeling in the world?

   _____

5. What kind of music do you relax to?

_____

6. What is the first thing you think of in the morning?

_____

7. If you had super powers that could change the world, what would you do?

_____

8. What's your favourite food?

_____

9. Do you subscribe to a monthly magazine?

_____

10. What's the most interesting thing you've ever done?

_____

11. What has been your life's defining moment up until now?

_____

12. If you could have any job you wanted, what would it be?

_____

13. What's your favourite sound?

_____

14. Who in your life makes you laugh the most?

_____

15. Which was your most successful year?

_____

16. What would you love people to say about you at a party?

_____

17. Is your glass half empty or half full?

_____

18. What's under your bed?

_____

19. What's your strongest quality?

_____

20. Where's your least favourite place to be?

_____

21. What makes you cry?

_____

22. What makes you angry?

_____

23. What makes you laugh?

_____

24. Who inspires you?

_____

25. If you could choose to live differently, how would you live?

_____

This isn't meant to be a laborious exercise, so fill it in quickly without thinking too much about your answers. Write whatever comes into your mind first. That way, your first answer is likely to be the one that's true.

Incidentally, these questions also act as great conversation openers at functions or parties where you need to make small talk. In the earlier chapter entitled 'The dating game', for instance, one of the tips to making easy small talk with strangers is to ask about them and their lives, and these questions give you ready-to-use opening lines that may lead on to all kinds of interesting conversations.

The connection we have with friends provides a vital and important facet to our lives, and our general wellbeing could be jeopardised if those contacts aren't kept up and looked after. If you've got no one to listen to you after a bad day or no one to laugh or share funny stories with, the lack of that close contact leaves a void that we'll naturally try to fill, and, yes, shopping fills it nicely – for a while!

If this questionnaire really isn't something you see yourself doing, then try to keep in touch with old friends in other ways. Send a card just for the sake of it, for instance. A quick, scribbled note to say you haven't forgotten they exist could mean so much to someone, and the fact that they haven't been in touch doesn't necessarily mean they're avoiding you or don't need you: they could have gone quiet because life isn't OK for them and they need someone to have a chat with. Your intuition is a great guide here. If someone pops into your mind for no reason at all, send them a text or email, give them a call or drop them a note in the post.

Take the time to nurture friendships and keep in touch with people you like. By filling in and swapping this questionnaire, you'll certainly learn all kinds of things about your friends and family and probably a few new things about yourself too.

Stop the world and get off

If life's taking its toll, you're at the end of your tether and you need to stop the world and get off for a while, you're going to love this.

This strategy is about giving in, letting go and just being. It's about being whatever you want to be – miserable, down, elated, indulgent. It's just about wrapping yourself up in a warm, soft blanket and letting all your worries and stresses disappear for a few hours. This girls, is how to stop the world and get off.

Giving in occasionally does wonders. We already know life is stressful; we already know we're leaned on by all kinds of people; we already know that we're intensely bad at looking after ourselves – and I don't mean hauling our backsides down to the gym or doing the latest celebrity yoga video. I'm talking about real soul nurturing here. I'm talking about creating pure moments of self-indulgent pleasure. I'm talking about creating the kinds of moments that mean the world carries on regardless, and, for once, just once, you're choosing not to be taken in by the hum of it.

Don't get me wrong: this isn't to be mistaken for an excuse to wander off into La-La Land for days on end, nor is it about hiding from the real world for ever. Strong, capable women like us *need* to be in this world, so you can't back out of it completely. What this strategy is about is giving yourself permission to take a very well-earned break every now and then. In fact, it's healthy to do so. We just keep trudging on though for another six or nine months until our next holiday – that's if we do go away at all. If we keep bottling up fears, tensions and worries, there will eventually be a very large explosion. It's that massive explosion waiting to happen that this strategy is meant to avoid, so make sure it doesn't *actually* happen. You probably already have minor explosions, snapping at people, spending too much and not caring where the money comes from, working too hard with the 'If I don't do it no one else will' ethic swirling around your brain – and none of that is pretty, empowering or useful.

In order to stop mistreating yourself, other people and your bank balance, you need special time to take special care of yourself. This is where you get to be your own nurturer and step out of the rat race for a while. This needn't be because no one else is going to look after you. You may well have lots of people who want to look after you, but asking for and accepting that help is sometimes very difficult. This strategy is about asking the woman who really knows what's best for you – and that's you.

Let this strategy give you the permission you need to give in to exhaustion and stop fighting the signs of not coping. This is about curling up, watching tear-jerking DVDs you've seen a thousand times, tucking unceremoniously into handmade choccies (that you bought for yourself) and snuggling up under the duvet on your sofa. Take off every trace of makeup, put on your saddest, most comfortable and least sexy pair of trackie bottoms, cuddle up with your favourite soft fleece, hold a tissue for comfort, take the phone off the hook and cry your eyes out – if that's what you need to do.

I'm already hearing you scream, 'I haven't got time', 'OK, where am I going to put the kids?' and 'Yeah, right, my family would give me permission to do that!' I'm not saying this is easy. I'm not saying that it won't need a bit of planning, but I *am* saying that it can be done. You just need to give yourself permission to do it first. This is your permission not to organise, not to be responsible, not to cook, not to be held accountable and most certainly not to look after anyone other than yourself.

Now, obviously, I am aware that this has to be done in controlled circumstances – that is, with children being cared for by someone responsible, and anyone else who lives with you being out for a few hours, but this is just one evening we're talking about, just one afternoon or just one morning, not a week, a month or a whole lifetime. It's just a short time for you to be allowed some privacy to 'feel' what's going on in your brain and allow yourself the space to heal when you feel you're losing your grip. Allow yourself the indulgence of stopping the world and you'll be far less likely to spiral out of control.

Kiera learned about the power of stopping the world when she sought coaching after she realised she was bursting into tears at the drop of a hat. When I spoke to Kiera, she hadn't had a holiday for four years; she'd been working solidly with only a few days off here and there; she'd been coping with illness that made her feel tired, tearful and negative; and what she told me she desperately craved was time alone just to cry her eyes out! So I asked her to go get it. She stopped crying and was silent for several minutes, staring blankly into space. She wiped her eyes, pulled herself up in her chair and smiled. 'OK, I will,' she said.

Kiera went home and organised various places for her family to be, packing them off without their realising why. Then she created in her mind exactly what she would need to do to make herself feel nurtured and taken care of. A week later the day came. She didn't shower, she stayed in her pyjamas all day, she watched her favourite DVD three times, drank numerous cups of tea, ate homemade chicken soup and cried – a lot. By the time her family were due home, she'd had a bubble bath, shaved her legs, done her hair and put on some fresh, clean clothes. She was ready for the world once more.

If you stopped the world for a few hours, what would you need to organise? What would make your perfect, self-indulgent day? What would you need to do to nurture your soul? If life's become one huge emotional and physical fight, decide to stop the fight and start again completely fresh the next day. It really does work.

Lost in time?

Does time panic you? Are you constantly telling people you haven't got time? If the clock rules your life and you don't feel dressed without your watch, then time could literally be taking over your life.

If your luxury item on a desert island would be a clock, then time could literally be taking you over. If being late is the worst thing that could happen to you, then this tip could just save your life.

Time is a funny thing. For children it drags and drags, but when we grow up it vanishes far too quickly. No sooner have you got your summer holiday photos developed than you're climbing up into the loft to sort through the Christmas decorations. Where does it all go? Why is it that in the twenty-first century we haven't yet worked out how to stop time going quite as fast?

One thing is for sure: time is constant and, however we fill it, everyone has the same amount. It's not prejudiced against the rich or poor. It's just there – and it's not going to budge. We just have to work around it.

Now there are always instances when time is imperative, but most of us panic and worry about it unnecessarily. First, time has two rules that every woman should know:

- Rule Number One – you have more time than you think;

- Rule Number Two – the more organised you are, the more time you create.

Most of my clients will admit to spending so much time worrying about how they're going to fit everything in that the fear of time reduces them to complete inaction and their precious time is wasted, never to be relived.

For Heather, punctuality was one of her biggest problems. She genuinely hated it when someone was late and yet *she* was always late. If you were late for Heather, instead of a warm welcome, you'd be likely to be greeted at the door by Godzilla with PMT! It infuriated her to such an extent and she got so stressed that it put her in a bad mood for the rest of the day.

This was turning into a huge issue for her. She felt guilty too, since she was constantly late for meetings, dental appointments and dinner with friends, but she found herself in the trap of time and didn't have the first clue why she was late for everything. When we spoke about it, it was obvious that Heather was always clock watching. She was absolutely convinced that, for a career woman, a wife and a mother, her workload was more than anyone else's. She'd flit from room to room and job to job both at work and in her personal life. Before she knew it, she'd have half-sorted piles of laundry draped around the house, beds half changed, the shopping half unpacked and the post half opened. She was so panicked by the thought of not having enough time that she tried to do all her jobs at once, ending up making very little progress anywhere.

The second thing that became obvious was that she appeared to be totally disorganised. Now I'm well aware that organisation isn't everyone's idea of fun but, if time is an issue, you'll create hours if you sit down and plan what you have to do and when you're going to do it.

You may think that Heather's time obsession is a bit dramatic but it was causing her a whole load of emotional anxiety and she realised it had to stop.

The first thing I asked her was, 'What needs to happen for you to stop panicking over the time?' Her answer? 'To take down all the clocks in my house!' She laughed at her own reply. It turns out that Heather loves clocks and had one in every single room. How is she ever going to be on time for anything without a clock? I hear you ask.

Actually, time wasn't the issue here: it was Heather's reaction to it that was the problem. If she couldn't clock-watch, she wouldn't panic. That was her theory, and she went home to put it to the test that very day. OK, her family hated it, but Heather was a changed woman and they loved that bit. Not only was she more relaxed than she'd been in years, but she ended up doing everything she needed to do in a much more focused manner, without the panic. Once she had got out of the habit of clock watching, she put some of the clocks back around the house and found that she really didn't look at them very often. Heather had learned to judge how long things took to complete and how long it would take her to get to places just by instinct, and finally she started to turn up to appointments on time.

There is a great test you can do to see just how good a judge of time you are. In true children's television style, all you need is a stopwatch and a friend! Get your friend to start the stopwatch while you carry on doing a normal everyday task. What you have to do is to try to estimate when one minute is up. Your friend will keep his or her eye firmly on the stopwatch and you'll be doing exactly what you always do while guessing when the minute is up. This is a great indication as to whether you really have a grip on time or whether it has a grip on you! If you're way off and two minutes have flown by before you've said 'stop', then my guess is that you're always late for things too. If you shout 'stop' after thirty seconds, on the other hand, you're never late but you're probably fearful of time and spend your time running around on pure adrenalin, rushing to get everything on your list done. If you're within ten seconds of the minute, you've got time pretty much sussed! Congratulations, you're the sort of person who knows that they can get everything done and you probably approach your life in a methodical and relaxed manner.

If you see a little bit of Heather in you and are starting to feel overwhelmed by time, then maybe you need to stop clock watching. Understand that you have more time than you think and get more organised. Another great tip for the list makers among you is to start your lists by writing a statement at the top in big letters that says, 'I have enough time to do everything I need'.

This reaffirms to your subconscious that you are capable of being efficient, effective and confident about delivering on time. If writing things down isn't your style, breathe deeply and slowly say to yourself, 'I have plenty of time, I have plenty of time …'

Don't get caught in the myth of the minute. Relax and take your time.

Cyber-struggles

Do you find yourself bickering via text messages? Do you argue over the email? Well, it's time to get back to the good old days and have it out face to face.

Call me old-fashioned but, in my view, if you're going to have an argument, you might as well do it face to face!

Text messaging and emails are all very well but there's one thing they just cannot replace: body language! When we speak to someone face to face, we don't just hear their words: we see their body language and hear the tone of their voice and whether, for example, they're being sarcastic or genuine. There are thousands of signals we receive, some of them conscious, most of them unconscious, about whether we like or trust that person, whether that person is lying or simply telling us what we want to hear. Nothing can make up for human interaction, however clever technology gets.

Ellen found out the hard way when she came to see me just after she had split up from her husband Steve. Ellen and Steve had been married for five years and had a daughter aged three. Family life was busy and both of them worked full-time, leaving their daughter with grand-parents during the day. Ellen and Steve worked shifts and would sometimes go for days just passing on the landing, as one was going to bed and the other was leaving for the childminder's and then work.

This put an immense strain on their relationship, which they had previously considered to be very good. They were a couple who had always had a policy of discussing issues properly, so, when they agreed to take on jobs that meant their daily routine would be disrupted for a while, they were sure their relationship was strong enough to withstand it.

During the past year, though, with both of them working unsocial shifts, their communication had been reduced to emails, text messages, notes on the kitchen table and answerphones. It worked reasonably well for the first few months: they left messages for each other when bills needed to be paid, when daughter Carrie was going to different people's houses and when the rubbish needed putting out, but they soon realised that the closeness in their relationship was missing. Ellen admits she became sarcastic; Steve retaliated with his notes; and slowly their relationship fell to the depths of arguing via text and emails and they were barely able to speak to each other.

Throughout all of this, neither Ellen nor Steve sat down properly and agreed to talk through their issues. Yes, time was an issue, but also, each was so hurt and angry at the other that each assumed the other wasn't much interested in building up the relationship again. Both assumed they had reached the point of no return.

It's so hard to get the right tone in an email, especially when writing it at work, since your communication may be intercepted or read by work colleagues. Text messages are even worse, because you have just a few characters to say exactly what you mean – and, between text language and speed text, you need a diploma to decipher some messages.

During the course of our sessions together, Ellen and Steve (who by now were living apart) agreed to meet and talk through some of the issues they had been faced with. It seems that a lot of misunderstandings had occurred during that period and it turns out that neither one of them really wanted a divorce. They agreed that, no matter how well paid their respective jobs were, they needed to be changed so they could spend some quality time together again as a family. Both Ellen and Steve have now changed jobs and spend every evening together as a result.

The tip? Talk to each other face to face. Use text messages and emails as communication by all means, but the really big stuff, the subjects that matter and the arguments should all be done face to face so you have the benefit of seeing people's facial expressions and their body language. It's important to be close enough to touch each other during difficult conversations. That way you'll be near enough to know whether the other person is upset. Otherwise, it's easy for one party to put up a façade while secretly raging underneath and blaming the other for not noticing.

Make sure you get it right, quit the Internet quarrelling and sort out your issues the old-fashioned way!

Sleeping beauty

Do you dread bedtime because you can't sleep? Are you so frustrated that everyone and everything in the house is snoring away and nothing is going to make you nod off? Is lack of sleep driving you slowly insane? Your answer could be here.

There are a million different reasons why people don't sleep properly at night. Young children, the snoring of partners and worry are among the most obvious and common complaints. However, what on earth do you do when these aren't the reasons? How come, when life seems to be running reasonably smoothly, when there don't seem to be any major dramas on the horizon and when you're genuinely shattered after a hard day, you still can't produce the zeds? What then?

Frustrating as it is, there are thousands of insomniacs around the globe getting up at ridiculous times of the morning, watching late-night repeats and putting the kettle on in an effort to make themselves tired enough to switch off.

Jess's lack of sleep came up in conversation during a discussion about her lack of organisational skills. Jess was constantly losing things; she took for ever to get out of the door with her daughter in the morning; she'd make endless lists, then lose them; and, as for the car keys, she'd been reduced to buying one of those key rings that play a tune when you whistle – so she couldn't lose it! Life for Jess was fractious to say the least, and she joked one day that it didn't help that she got no more than three hours of sleep each night. There's no way most of us could function on that little sleep. Everyone's sleep patterns and needs are different, but three hours a night is generally far too little to be able to function as a normal human being.

I asked Jess to describe her bedroom to me. I already knew that her life was chaotic and I wondered whether her bedroom was just as bad – and it was. It wasn't some-where that she liked to spend time. It was in need of redec-orating, the curtains were old, the chair in the corner was a hoarding place for clothes, the washing basket was also in the room, making it smell stale and her bedside table was cluttered with makeup, perfume bottles, moisturisers and toners. There wasn't a clear surface anywhere and the floor was littered with the magazines that she would read through a wakeful night. It was only when Jess started to describe her surroundings that it became clear to her that she needed to tidy up and clean up!

Your bedroom should be a haven of tranquillity, decorated in restful colours and illuminated with gentle lighting. The window should be easily accessible to freshen the room every day and linen should be cotton, so it breathes properly. It should be the one place in the house where you feel relaxed and comfortable in your private space. When you sleep, your body is still at work. Your body uses that downtime to repair and renew cells, so it's vital for your health and strength that you allow your body to sleep properly.

For the perfect bedroom, make sure it's clutter-free and easy to clean. If it helps, take away the obvious clutter zones such as chairs and laundry baskets. Make sure your bedroom isn't overloaded with furniture, and clear your bedside table. The essentials are fresh water each night, a pen and paper to write down any worries you have racing around your mind, a good book to relax with and some essential oils such as lavender to promote blissful sleep.

Jess made a lot of changes to her bedroom and all it cost her was a bit of time and a pot of paint. Now she feels much more able to relax and drifts off to sleep much more quickly than she ever used to. Her sleep pattern had been disrupted for many years and, although she'll never need ten hours a night, she is getting at least five or six quality hours of sleep and feels more organised as a result.

If you had to use one word to describe your bedroom, what word would you choose? Restful? Passionate? Warm? Inviting? Sexy, even? Perhaps it's more like messy, jumbled and dated! If that's the case, make this weekend the one you set aside to get your bedroom sorted out. Throw the windows and the curtains open, go through old papers and magazines – and be ruthless. Throw away out-of-date perfume, old creams and potions; clear out everything from under the bed (yes I do mean everything!); get the hoover out; rearrange the furniture if you like, but have a thorough clean up and make bedtime your favourite time of the day.

OK, girls, put your money where your mouth is!

Wouldn't you love to be able to say that you gave your life a complete overhaul as a result of reading this book? Perhaps you've diligently read hundreds of self-help books but have never been able to gather the enthusiasm or find the willpower to do any of the exercises? Wouldn't you love this time to be different, for your friends to be in total awe of your success and 'togetherness'? Then here's your chance.

In this final chapter, it's time for you to put your money where your mouth is. Take the opportunity to put some of these tips into practice and become your very own success story. What you've done by buying and reading this book is make a conscious decision to do something different in your everyday life, to do something more positive and satisfying with your existence on this planet. If slogging your way to work to do a job that you don't like or working for people who make you feel bad about yourself isn't your idea of living with excitement and passion, then what is?

In this book, you've been given the tools to be able to make a conscious decision today about the way you live your life, a chance to make the massive decision to change your life for the better. Work out today, this lunchtime or this evening what you would need to change in your life to make *you* the success story and to make others envy your lifestyle, your zest for living, your energy and enthusiasm even on the dullest day. Forget seasonal affective disorder, shrug off depression and rid yourself of the financial complications that make you feel inadequate. This is it, girls: this is your big chance, and you have no choice but to take this wonderful opportunity in both hands and cherish it for all it's worth.

If you were attracted to the title of this book because it sounded like you or if you read it in the hope that it would finally spur you into moving your life forward in a more focused direction, this last chapter is probably the most important one you could read. This is about doing something for yourself, taking in the knowledge you've read both here and in other books, taking the tips, the strategies and the inspiration that your subconscious mind has so readily soaked up and working out how you can fit these new skills and views into your lifestyle, so that it becomes slicker, more enjoyable, more relaxing and more profitable, financially as well as emotionally.

Perhaps you've had to face up to a few home truths while reading this; perhaps you've noticed patterns of how you've frittered away money on things that ultimately don't matter. Perhaps you've realised that other things in your life – your relationship, your health, your career – just aren't giving you the satisfaction they should and that shopping has been the emotional crutch that sees you through the day and prevents you from bursting into tears everywhere.

Perhaps you've finally had enough. You've had your 'moment of clarity' (they say everyone gets one!) and, as a result, you've decided that from now on life's going to be different and *you're* going to be different. Maybe this has helped you to take a long overdue look at your priorities, to delve into the things that really matter, such as relationships, health, adventure, communication, living with spirit and passion and, of course, your own self-development as a capable, intelligent woman. These are the things that make huge differences to the quality of life and, while a bit of Gucci never did anyone any harm, it's not what turns the world around and your world won't stop turning if you decide to stop spending excessively. One thing is sure: no one ever said on their death bed that they wished they'd redecorated in this season's colours one last time, that they'd ironed more socks or that they wish they'd been able to afford a sportier car! When it comes down to it, those just aren't the things that matter.

We are constantly hearing stories of how near-death experiences or the death of a loved one wakes people up and gives them the jolt they need to start living a more fulfilling and exciting life. Well, how about choosing not to wait until you've experienced near-death? What about choosing to let this very moment be your wake-up call? Whatever your age, financial status or daily routine, there is always more time to spend with family than you think; there are infinitely more ways that you could show loved ones how much they mean to you; there are a million and one healthier ways to live your life and expand your potential. Take every chance you get to experience the real riches of life.

There are a few more questions that, if you're serious about making changes, will help you to focus your intentions. This requires no more than grabbing a pencil and scribbling down the answers that come to mind first, then acting on them. It's that focus that will ultimately give you the push you need to bring lasting and positive change into your life. Don't waste precious time presuming that you'll sort things out eventually – this *is* your eventually! Be determined to make changes now. Imagine that I'm sitting by your side, metaphorically holding your hand, giving you the courage to change the direction of your life in any way you choose. If I were sitting next to you, these would be some of the questions I'd be asking you. These are questions that will help to give you direction, clarity and focus in your next move. Take a deep breath, grab that pencil and take a few minutes to have a think, here goes.

What have you learned from reading this book?

_____

_____

_____

What or who in this book has particularly inspired you?

_____

_____

_____

What has surprised you?

_____

_____

_____

OK, girls, put your money where your mouth is!

What have you learned about yourself?

_____

_____

_____

Which chapter has been of most help to you?

_____

_____

_____

What have you decided to do differently as a result of reading *Behind with the Mortgage and Living off Plastic*?

_____

_____

_____

What in your life makes you brim over with pride?

_____

_____

_____

What in your life makes you feel exhilarated and want to shout from the rooftops?

_____

_____

_____

What in your life makes you sad and frustrated?

_____

_____

_____

What keeps you trapped in a sad and frustrated mindset?

_____

_____

_____

What do you want more of in your life?

_____

_____

_____

What are you going to do today to make sure you get more of what you love in your life, so that tomorrow you wake up brimming with passion, babbling with excitement and wondering where this renewed gusto for life actually came from?

_____

_____

_____

Now go do it!

Whatever it is, whatever you've written, make this your life's defining moment, make this your wake-up call and decide to do everything in your power to weed out the stuff that makes you miserable and keep in more of the stuff that makes you glow with exhilaration. Once you make the changes, you'll never look back – well, only to gloat occasionally about just how fabulous life really is now!

Have fun!

Lynette x

Contact Lynette Allen

For further details about one-to-one coaching offered by Lynette, visit www.lynetteallen.co.uk

Tracklist for accompanying CD

1. Introduction **02:42**
2. A woman's work is never done – or is it? **04:53**
3. Decluttering commitments **04:53**
4. Your fifties are your twenties – with style! **06:56**
5. Body confidence tips just for girls **05:01**
6. Lost in time? **06:37**
7. Get started right here, right now **05:06**
8. The dating game **05:25**
9. How do you react? **03:19**
10. Sleeping beauty **04:56**
11. OK, girls, put your money where your mouth is! **07:56**